Dedicated to all the people in the world.
For many are invited, but few are chosen (Matthew 22:14).

YHWH Is Calling

Leora Lavan

The Pennant Has Been Mounted!
The Trumpet of the Lord Is Playing!
The Return of the Lord Is Approaching!

1. Edition

Copyright © 2021 Hoshiana Mission

Publisher: Hoshiana Mission, St. Michel, Finland

Producer: BoD - Books on Demand, Norderstedt, German

Translation: Mathilda / Tekstipro.fi, Kayade Oy, Tallinn, Estonia

Book cover painting: ElisaR, St. Michel, Finland

Book cover design: Hoshiana Mission, St. Michel, Finland

Scripture taken from the New King James Version.

Copyright © 1982 by Thomas Nelson, Inc.

ISBN 978-952-69508-4-6 (sid.)
ISBN 978-952-69508-5-3 (EPUB)

Contents

Foreword

"And it shall come to pass That whoever calls on the name of
the Lord Shall be saved. For in Mount Zion and in
Jerusalem there shall be deliverance,
As the Lord has said, Among the remnant
whom the Lord calls."
Joel 2:32

When I asked the Lord in a prayer for the name for His book, which
this is, the Lord gave the words "YHWH is calling". During the
second silent prayer, the Lord continued His instruction: "Return my
name YHWH to His own ones' lips. Declare, as His trumpet, that the
age has begun when those who cry out for His name will be saved.
Remind the people of how He told His elect to listen to His
instructions sent through His messengers even before He gave His
Holy Word."

The task might have sounded impossible if I had not already been
able to see and experience how the Almighty still these days
continues to act in accordance with His Holy Word. Had the Lord not
back then chosen from the earthly modest conditions in the middle of
the remote regions, the breeder of the sheep, Amos, to proclaim a

serious message to the leaders of the ancient people of Israel, I would have been deeply amazed at the Almighty's choice to approach, with similar requests, a woman who has already been battered in life in the middle of Finland's wooded outlying areas.

I also got to experience the truth of how the Almighty sees directly into people's hearts and answers questions that the human being has not even uttered aloud yet. To dispel my doubts about my suitability for the use of the Almighty, the Lord confirmed the call by continuing the teaching through His Spirit. Lovingly, the Lord explained why He wants the gospel for Easter 2021/5781 to be proclaimed to the nations precisely in the middle of a remote village of a remote nation. Just as Jesus (Yeshua in the original text) approached Jerusalem at one time as the beginning of a significant new age, riding to Jerusalem on a donkey foal liberated from a remote village, the birth and liberation of a donkey foal would precede the Lord's return to Jerusalem. This secret, concerning our own age, hidden in the Scriptures about the donkey foal which birth and release we are blessed to be witnessing with our own eyes, I try to describe in the first chapter of the book in the form of a letter sent to my dear friend, as prompted by the Lord.

In the following sections of the book, I write about the more serious part related to the gospel to the elders of the Jewish and Christian congregations. Our God, YHWH, wants to see His beloved daughters of Zion and the gentile representatives that have joined them, once again, together as joyful and equally respectful sisters celebrating the celebration associated with the great salvation work of His Son.

As a result of the apostasy of the nation, both daughters of Zion had to be expelled by the Almighty from the Promised Land in ancient times. One of the daughters also received a certificate of divorce by the Lord, but at the same time a promise of retaining grace and re-engagement during the next generations before the day of the

Lord. Both daughters have been tested by the Lord, and for both daughters He has set their own stumbling blocks to be written in world history. However, as a part of the gospel, I am pleased to declare that we have arrived at that time of grace and re-engagement of the daughter who received the certificate of divorce.

Christian congregations (descendants of brethren Ephraim) are therefore called by YHWH around the world to return from heresies to the original covenant with Him. YHWH allowed the eyes and ears of Christians to open first to receive Jesus as the Savior fulfilling the prophecies of the Scriptures. However, in order to be an equal Father to His children and to prevent His daughter from boasting, YHWH allowed the cover of significant doctrinal delusions, taken by an ancient emperor that would remain onto the eyes of Christians for about 1,700 years. This cover that the Lord placed on Christians for a period of time has been seen in past centuries as anti-Semitism by even major Christian reformers, such as Martin Luther.

I am pleased to announce that the Lord will remove this cover from the eyes of all Christians who, in the age beginning with the trumpeting of the Almighty, are ready to respond to the Lord's call. Because of the above, the gospel also includes a serious ordeal for Christian congregations. Which of us are ready to admit missteps and repent? Which of us are ready to respond to YHWH's call to learn from the Jewish brothers and sisters about their ways, cherished for millenia, of spending the biblical Sabbath and the Feast of Tabernacles? Which of us are ready to restore God's Holy Word to a higher authority than the decisions taken by the people?

The Jews, on the other hand, have had the privilege of being a daughter (Sister Judah), to whom YHWH did not issue the certificate of divorce in addition to the ancient deportation order. Indeed, Jews have had the privilege of celebrating the holy day consecrated to the

Lord, set by the Almighty as a sign of the covenant for the Lord Sebaot, all past centuries at the original time and enjoying a joyful family connection, just as our Savior did. However, receiving the saving gospel of our Savior was set as a touchstone for the daughter of Judah for millennia. The era of the gospel thus includes its own test for the daughter Judah. YHWH urges Jews to forgive the grave transgressions of Christian brothers and sisters in their past centuries of delusion and to open their hearts to the gospel message of Jesus as the promised Savior.

What a great and loving Almighty Heavenly Father we have! He is a fair and equitable Father to His children. He loves showing goodness and setting boundaries. Jews and Christians are His beloved children, whom He now wants to go hand in hand to praise and thank the Lord, as well as to cry for help again in the middle of the tribulations of the age. Both daughters need each other to survive the trials of the era that has begun.

Let us open our hearts to listen to the instructions, commandments, and loving warnings of the Almighty, as He has urged in His Holy Word to His elect to do, during the earthly journey.

> *"For I did not speak to your fathers, or command*
> *them in the day that I brought them out of*
> *the land of Egypt, concerning burnt offerings*
> *or sacrifices. But this is what I commanded them,*
> *saying, 'Obey My voice, and I will be your God,*
> *and you shall be My people. And walk in*
> *all the ways that I have commanded you,*
> *that it may be well with you.'"*
> *Jeremiah 7:22-23*

Hosanna! The Lord, please help us to hear Your voice and walk Your way to salvation!

Part 1
Gospel for Easter 2021/5781

"All inhabitants of the world and dwellers
on the earth: When he lifts up a banner on the mountains,
you see it; And when he blows a trumpet, you hear it."
Isaiah 18:3

As prompted by the Lord, I am publishing a letter I wrote to a friend for wider distribution:

My dear friend, I am completely excited for matters for which the Spirit gave me a revelation in recent weeks. This time of Easter is special throughout God's Global Plan of Salvation.

On the first Easter (Passover) of humankind, the deliverance of God's elect from Egypt was at a turning point and God's own ones were able to avoid the punishment Egypt was facing by brushing the door frames with the blood of a sacrificed lamb. Since then, the blood of the Easter lambs has been shed every year in memory of the deliverance of slavery in Egypt and the deliverance of death of the firstborns.

Centuries later, Jesus was hung on the cross right on Easter as the sacrificial lamb of all humankind. After that, sacrificial animals were no longer needed to atone for sins. Everyone who would receive Jesus as their Saviour and follow Him would be cleansed and saved by the blood shed by Jesus at Calvary. From then on, instead of sacrificial animals, the steers of the lips would be sacrificed to God as thanksgiving sacrifices (prayers from the lips, sacrifices of praise and thanksgiving, Hos. 14: 3, Heb. 10: 10-12, Heb. 13: 15-16, Rom. 12: 1).

After having afflicted, for several weeks, the revelation I received from the Spirit and after having received heart-reassuring confirmations from the Lord, I dare to proclaim the gospel as the Lord prompted. This Easter, there is another turning point in God's plan for the salvation of humankind. The Spirit of the Lord in his revelation revealed to me that we have arrived at a time when the Lord will lower his pennant to the mountains as a sign for the inhabitants on the Earth and the trumpets will be playing by the mouth of the prophets.

I am pleased to announce, with the Lord's prompting, that this time of prophecy in the book of Isaiah has begun!

In this beginning age, He will complete the formerly banished pardon of the remnant of Israel, and will eventually reunite Judah & Ephraim (Ezek. 37, Zechariah 9: 9-10: 12 and many other places in the Word). By raising this pennant and playing the Lord's trumpet, the end of the age of grace has begun. As it is written, with the descendants of Judah and Israel a large number of the pagans who joined them (people from numerous different Christian congregations) will be saved.

During this age, nations will also have to choose whether they want to be the nation of sheep or goats on the approaching day of the Lord's return. The events of the following years in Finland will be a testimony to the power of God and a sign for many other nations to move into this era.

Introduction to the Revelation of the Spirit

You know, we have the habit of saying evening prayer in the evenings and then I usually switch on an about 20 min clip on the application 'Raamattu kannesta kanteen' (Bible from cover to cover). The voice of radio Pastor Norvanto, who explains the Bible, is so pleasantly calm that it is rarely in the evenings that I manage to listen to the teachings more than halfway through before I fall asleep. I warmly recommend this habit. When you focus on listening to the Word of the Bible and the associated explanations of secrets and things, your brain will not end up thinking of uncomfortable earthly things that slow down you falling asleep.

One evening a few weeks ago, I was amazed as choosing the program to listen to when I was prompted by the Lord to listen specifically to the teachings of the book of Hosea. I was not excited about the idea and I meant to choose something completely different. However, I immediately received a new call to only choose the book of Hosea that night. At that point I could only say "Alright, alright, My Heavenly Father..". I had previously read that book around two years ago and back then I did not understand at all why the Word urged the Prophet Hosea to choose a fornicating wife for himself. However, I noticed that when the Lord had meanwhile opened the meaning of the constellation of Revelation in 2017 and the connection to the birth of the Finnish nation that expulsion of the northern tribes of Israel in general has, the fornication discussed in the book of Hosea began to unfold in a completely new way. To my amazement, the Lord, then again through His own Spirit, continued the teaching of things to me. Surely the Spirit has now spoken of the revelation I shared somewhere in the world to some of his other servants, but I am pleased to be involved in sharing this secret revealed by God after afflicting it and being prompted by the Spirit to publish it.

My joy is great in proclaiming this good news concerning the whole Earth, because, as you know, I will soon have to, with as heavy heart as Elijah and Amos once did to Ephraim, bring to the attention of the people of Finland yet God's last serious warning about the nation's and the country's apostasy. Today, however, I can only focus on the good news of Easter time!

You probably remember from school times the frequent description of how Jesus rides a donkey to Jerusalem for Easter. For how many decades have we sung 'Tiellä ken vaeltaa, ken aasilla ratsastaa' (Who walks on the road, who rides on a donkey) in Finland on Advents and Palm Sundays which ends with the blaring Hosanna, Hosanna (meaning the Lord, please help, save)!

My dear friend, a few weeks ago the Holy Spirit gave me a mind-blowing revelation about the resemblance of the donkey foal used by Jesus to our present age. Likewise, the Holy Spirit made a revelation that the same thing is related to why He blessed the people of Finland with a female-shaped land in the last century.

Although I only can scratch the whole unit here, which would certainly easily take two hours if I explained it face to face, I cannot wait but share this "secret" of the donkey foal with you, even a little bit.

However, first I rehearse a little bit of the background because I do not remember how much I have shared with you about the magnitude of the division of ancient Israel in God's Plan of Salvation regarding our time.

The Deportation of Ancient Divided Israel

As I can recall, I wrote to you earlier about how the northern and southern states of ancient divided Israel drifted into renunciation of keeping the Word of God. As a consequence, God banished these "unbelieving" siblings of Zion each of them to their directions:

*"The Lord said also to me in the days of
Josiah the king: 'Have you seen what backsliding
Israel has done? She has gone up on every high
mountain and under every green tree,
and there played the harlot. And I said,
after she had done all these things,
'Return to Me.' But she did not return.
And her treacherous sister Judah saw it.
Then I saw that for all the causes for
which backsliding Israel had committed adultery,
I had put her away and given her a certificate
of divorce; yet her treacherous sister Judah
did not fear, but went and played
the harlot also. So it came to pass,
through her casual harlotry,
that she defiled the land and committed
adultery with stones and trees.
And yet for all this her treacherous sister*

Judah has not turned to Me with her
whole heart, but in pretense,' says the Lord."
Jeremiah 3:6-10

The nation of the southern state of Judah (the present Jews and those who joined them, including the Benjamin tribe of that time) was once again able to return to Israel and build another temple which was destroyed according to Jesus' revelation after Jesus' death.

Some time after the death of Jesus, even the nation of Judah was again deported, this time around the world. As a significant sign of the progress of God's Plan of Salvation as it is written, we have, in the last century, been able to verify the rebirth of the state of Israel and observe how the Jews, according to the Word, will once again return around the world to the Promised Land.

Nevertheless, the significance of the deportation of the northern 10 tribes deported around 700 BC in our present era is less well known. The tribe of Ephraim was the largest tribe in the northern state of ancient Israel and therefore the northern part is often spoken of as Ephraim in the Word (in some places Israel, but in some places Israel is also used to describe the whole nation descended from Jacob as well as spiritually united Israel). Living in that northern kingdom before the expulsion became very unjustified, immoral, and fearless of God, so God finally announced through His prophets that He would carry out the expulsion. For the case of your beloved ones, please do remember everything that I have told so far about the challenging task of mine to describe the connection between the current state of Finland and the state that led to the ancient punishments of Ephraim. It must be remembered that the loss of the land did not come as a surprise to Ephraim, but through His prophets God had warned centuries earlier of the consequences of apostasy when he arrived in the Promised Land. Ephraim was banished, and the book of Jeremiah describes how the sister of the unfaithful southern state follows in the path of apostasy to the pity of the Lord.

Deprived People Are Wild Donkeys

"Israel is swallowed up; Now they are among
the Gentiles Like a vessel in which is no pleasure.
For they have gone up to Assyria,
Like a wild donkey alone by itself;
Ephraim has hired lovers."
Hosea 8:8-9

Regarding the understanding of the matter related to the donkey foal in the Easter tableau, it should be noted from the Word how God calls these expelled nations, e.g. in the book of Hosea, as wild asses (the verses related to Judah among others Jer. 2:24-28).

As a significant difference between the deportations of the nations is also to be noted the fact that God announced to the northern state of Israel that he would give a dissertation (Jer. 3:8) is also to be noted. Unlike the case of the southern state of Judah, God broke (marital) covenant with the nation of northern Israel. You probably remember God having made a (marital) covenant with all the members of the tribes of Israel and the strangers who joined them on Mount Sinai as the Israelites wandered from Egypt in the wilderness toward the Promised Land after liberation. Less well known is the related strengthening of the covenant with the sworn covenant described in 5. Deuteronomy 29. This covenant text and the following chapter 30 are worth being read carefully because even from them it can be seen that God already at that time knew the apostasy of Israel coming true. At the same time, it is comforting to read how the Lord already then, in the first books of the Bible also describes the pardon at the end of time and how He then picks up and reassembles His own into one group of nations Himself.

In order to understand completely the symbolic significance of riding a donkey foal, it is important to remember that God in His holiness follows His own instructions & the law He has given meticulously accurately. God, therefore, is not about to re-engage with the people (wild asses) to whom he gave the dissertation. After all, our God forbids remarriage with a wife to whom the husband has already given a certificate of divorce. (This provision is given so that divorces would not be taken that easily but the finality of the divorce from the point of view of obeying God would be taken into consideration. Those who unconsciously ended up doing this way, be at peace. As both The Old and The New Testament brings up that God, in watching our mistakes, takes into account whether the sin has been committed consciously or unknowingly, so be at peace.).

It can be read at many places in Word how the pardon of the northern nation would take place at the end of time during following generations. So one day the foal of that wild ass nation will experience what is written about this pardon and it will also have a connection to the approach of the day of the return of the Lord. Are you already starting to see the connection to the donkey foal from a new perspective?

As God's way of conducting things in his plan of salvation so that historical events repeat themselves in the corresponding stages of the Global Plan of Salvation is added to this the following places of the Word may open up an understanding of the connection of the donkey riding to the approach of Jesus' second coming.

"Now when they drew near Jerusalem,
and came to Bethphage, at the Mount of Olives,
then Jesus sent two disciples, saying to them,
'Go into the village opposite you,
and immediately you will find a donkey tied, and a colt
with her. Loose them and bring them to Me.
And if anyone says anything to you, you shall say,
'The Lord has need of them, and immediately
he will send them.' All this was done that it might
be fulfilled which was spoken by the prophet,
saying: 'Tell the daughter of Zion,
Behold, your King is coming to you,
Lowly, and sitting on a donkey,
A colt, the foal of a donkey.''"
Matthew 21:1-5

"Rejoice greatly, O daughter of Zion!
Shout, O daughter of Jerusalem!
Behold, your King is coming to you;
He is just and having salvation,
Lowly and riding on a donkey,
A colt, the foal of a donkey. I will cut
off the chariot from Ephraim And
the horse from Jerusalem; The battle
bow shall be cut off. He shall speak
peace to the nations; His dominion shall be
'from sea to sea, And from the River to
the ends of the earth.'"
Zechariah 9:9-10

Although Jesus rode a concrete donkey foal when he first came to Jerusalem, and many already received Him as the promised Messiah and King, the time did not fully fulfil Zechariah's prophecy of taking over the kingdom of the world with the beginning of the time of peace. The prophecy will therefore not be fully fulfilled until Jesus returns to the Mount of Olives as it is written. This time, as well, a donkey foal would be involved in Jesus' arrival in Jerusalem. The foal part is carried out by that pardoned group of ancient descendants of Israel, which has been joined by many people, including people from pagan nations. Now consider the description of the gospel about the Easter time events from another perspective. It should be noted that the mare of the donkey, also said to be on the yoke, was released together with the foal, and both were brought to the Lord. It was only after this revelation given by the Spirit that I understood why the book of Job also referred to the humanization of the wild donkey foal!

"For an empty-headed man will be wise, when
a wild donkey's colt is born a man."
Job 11:12

Just think! This is what a wonderful book of secrets the Bible is! All the future happenings are revealed there, but deliberately some of the secrets are partially hidden, behind some studying with the Spirit, to be revealed at the prompting of the Lord when the time is ripe enough for it.

And the amazing things will not end here. Next, I would like to share with you briefly how all this relates to our days and the form of the Finnish Maiden.

Childbirth as a Sign of the Time of Grace

There are numerous verses in the Word about the pardon of Israel and the return of the descendants of the ancient people of Judah at the end of time. I will raise just one verse here, from which we can land on the connection of the donkey metaphor to today's events in Finland and in the world.

> *"Therefore He shall give them up,*
> *Until the time that she who is in labor*
> *has given birth; Then the remnant of His brethren*
> *Shall return to the children of Israel.*
> *And He shall stand and feed His flock*
> *In the strength of the Lord, In the majesty*
> *of the name of the Lord His God;*
> *And they shall abide, For now He shall*
> *be great To the ends of the earth;"*
> *Micah 5:3-4*

Suddenly, childbirth may bring to mind the idea that the Old Testament verse would refer to the still-prophesied birth of Jesus at that time. After all, Jesus also said in the Gospels to a Canaanite woman belonging to the pagans (when she asked for a miracle of the Spirit for her daughter, eventually receiving it):

"But He answered and said, 'I was not sent
except to the lost sheep of the house of Israel.'"
Matthew 15:24

At the time of Jesus' birth, the nation of northern Israel had been banished centuries earlier, and only some of the Jews of Judah had faith that Jesus was indeed the Messiah promised by the Old Testament. The suspicion of the Jews was understandable, as the people expected a concrete king to take power who would restore justice and peace to the state of the ancient nation. However, at the time of his first coming, Jesus glorified a very different future kingdom of the heavenly kingdom than the earthly kingdom expected at the time. From the Gospels, however, it is verifiable that Jesus fulfilled the prophecies of the Old Testament Scriptures concerning the coming Messiah, although some of them He is about to fulfil at His Second Coming.

Like the prophecy of the book of Zechariah about the arrival of Jesus on the back of a donkey foal to take the kingdom, the verse of the book of Micah above has not yet been fully fulfilled. The birth referred to in the verse of Micah above is indicated by Revelation chapter 12.

"Now a great sign appeared in heaven:
a woman clothed with the sun, with the moon
under her feet, and on her head a garland of
twelve stars. Then being with child, she cried out
in labor and in pain to give birth."
Revelation 12:1-2

Although the forces of perdition have stolen celestial bodies through astrology for the worship of space spirits and idols, believers must remember that the celestial bodies were originally given to believers as signs of night, day, months, years, and eras.

My dear friend, every believer should be aware of that the constellation of the Book of Revelation came true in the sky on September 23, 2017 (there is a program explaining this in more detail in the supplementary materials). But the congregations seem to be asleep in following the signs given by the Lord. How can the members of the congregations be awake and bleach their clothes if they are caressed by the elders of the congregation to sleep by closing their eyes from the signs of the Lord, or, in the worst case, they are even urged to splash yet more dirt on their clothes (referring, among other things, to the transformation of things that God has determined to be sins into human decisions as part of the preaching ear scabies described in the Word).

The Feminine Form of Finland as a Sign on the World Map

I dare to write you the following text with full assurance of faith and courage because I have got myself an access to that great grace of the Lord. You know my long and challenging course of faith from the confirmation through the school of God to the rebirth of the Lord a few years ago. However, I do not remember mentioning to You how, blissfully yet unaware of that realization of the sign of Revelation chapter 12 in the sky and its significance, God appeared to me at that time with very special revelations. First, the Lord began to speak to me, an ordinary member of the Evangelical Lutheran Church, about the prompt to restore the holy day I had spend every Sunday to the place of the original Sabbath.

As a member of the Evangelical Lutheran Church, I was perhaps already at the time amazed about the act of the Holy Spirit itself, because I had not heard of the gifts of grace spoken as part of a believer's life, let alone seen it in action. As I cautiously approached a few people on the subject, I was amazed to find that God had begun to address other people across the church boundaries in the same years. The revelation of the Lord was so strong that if He had not prepared people with a similar understanding within the Evangelical

Lutheran Church, I would probably have had to change the church to follow God's call. However, God's plan is different. Although in Finland too, as in many other countries, as a consequence of democracy drifted into apostasy, have already many persons been selected to the spiritual leadership services of the Evangelical Lutheran Church to preach about the ear scabies that the people wish instead of the Holy Will announced by Abraham, Isaac and Jacob's God, Yahweh, will our God still give our church an opportunity. As well as to other Christian congregations, is time to humble ourselves back to the apostolic proclamation of the Word.

After all, God set the Sabbath as an eternal sign between Him and His own. Jesus also conscientiously celebrated the Sabbath although He renewed and took a stand on a few issues, adding a broader perspective to the New Covenant onto the Old Covenant. The Almighty's premise to first speak to me about that was therefore well understandable. It is also quite logical when understanding to have arrived at the age when God has mercy and re-engages with Israel (referring here specifically to ancient Ephraim, who had received a certificate of divorce which in the Word is sometimes called Israel alongside Judah). If God restores the covenant He has broken, then, of course He will also restore His Holy Sabbath as a sign of the covenant. I was urged to publish a more detailed account of that matter for the elders of the congregations, and that's why, my friend, I will not open it up to you in more detail here.

However, the Sabbath was not the only thing the Lord dealt with. As God's guidance progressed, there was no ambiguity about how God had begun to address people in various churches within Scandinavia and around the world about how much of His Word has been changed by human decisions over the centuries to something other than what the Word says. Over the centuries, several Reformers had been involved, but now the Lord Himself seemed to be acting directly through His Spirit, speaking to different congregation members about the same things across congregation boundaries, across borders of countries and continents. However, I still did not realize at the time that I myself was a part of that birth of a wild donkey foal, to which even the Word describes God as associating the restoration of His own to original obedience to His Word. I would not have believed even myself yet back then how we really have moved into an age when the age of grace is approaching its ending point.

> *"Therefore, behold, I will allure her,*
> *Will bring her into the wilderness,*
> *And speak comfort to her. I will give her*
> *her vineyards from there, And the Valley of Achor*
> *as a door of hope; She shall sing there,*
> *As in the days of her youth, As in the day*
> *when she came up from the land of Egypt.*
> *'And it shall be, in that day,' Says the Lord,*
> *'That you will call Me 'My Husband,'*
> *And no longer call Me 'My Master,''"*
> *Hosea 2:14-16*

As I pointed out in my article last autumn after having listened to teachings of Pekka Sartola on the topic, the modern genetic technology has proven to have surprisingly many descendants of the ancient people of northern Israel in Scandinavia, as well as, of course, the descendants of the people of the ancient southern state of Judah. As I also pointed out in my previous text, the amazingly beautiful shape of a female maiden of Finland is by no means a coincidence. Also, it is no coincidence in the world of our God either that this bridesmaid will be born on the world map at the same time as Israel after the break of millenniums.

In his revelation, the Lord revealed that the form of female appearing on the world map, on the other hand, was an earthly sign of the approach of the time by having appeared a woman in the signs of heaven in Revelation 12. At the same time, on the other hand, it can be understood as illustrating the re-engagement of the remnant of Israel that happens after that sign seen in heaven. There is a time in God's Global Plan of Salvation for the remnant of Israel, to dance again as a joyful pardoned bridesmaid. It is by no means a coincidence that the edges of the north and the joyful carnival dance are separately highlighted in the Word:

> "'At the same time,' says the Lord,
> 'I will be the God of all the families of Israel,
> and they shall be My people.' Thus says the Lord:
> 'The people who survived the sword
> Found grace in the wilderness —
> Israel, when I went to give him rest.'
> The Lord has appeared of old to me, saying:
> 'Yes, I have loved you with an everlasting love;
> Therefore with lovingkindness I have drawn you.
> Again I will build you, and you shall be rebuilt,
> O virgin of Israel! You shall again be adorned
> with your tambourines, And shall go forth
> in the dances of those who rejoice.
> You shall yet plant vines on the mountains
> of Samaria; The planters shall plant and
> eat them as ordinary food. For there
> shall be a day When the watchmen
> will cry on Mount Ephraim,
> 'Arise, and let us go up to Zion,
> To the Lord our God.' For thus says the Lord:
> 'Sing with gladness for Jacob,
> And shout among the chief of the nations;

Proclaim, give praise, and say,
'O Lord, save Your people,
The remnant of Israel!' Behold, I will
bring them from the north country,
And gather them from the ends of the earth,
Among them the blind and the lame,
The woman with child And the one
who labors with child, together;
A great throng shall return there. They shall
come with weeping, And with supplications
I will lead them. I will cause them to walk
by the rivers of waters, In a straight way
in which they shall not stumble; For I am a Father
to Israel, And Ephraim is My firstborn. '
Hear the word of the Lord, O nations,
And declare it in the isles afar off, and say,
'He who scattered Israel will gather him,
And keep him as a shepherd does his flock.''''
Jeremiah 31:1-10

I want to, and I am allowed to stick today only to proclaiming the good news of the birth of the donkey foal. However, I warn against thinking that, because Finland was given the grace to act as a visible sign to the nations on earth, it could do anything without responsibility for things in the eyes of God. Despite the obtained beautiful appearance and the beginning of the independent era blessed by God, God cannot and has not ignored Finland's current state of apostasy because of its holiness. Just like all nations through the ages, the people of Finland have been able to choose for themselves whether to remain obedient to God's Word and keep the blessings or to choose the path of apostasy and tearful shaking.

The End of the Age of Grace Has Begun

My dear friend, I know your faith in the existence of some higher power, but you have not yet received Jesus into your heart as your Saviour. Oh, if only I could give the faith to you like this.

After the confirmation, I lived for about 20 years in a misconception of salvation. I had been misled that baptism, church membership, and confirmation were a guarantee of belonging to the Lord's own ones and for a place in heaven. I was prompted by God to put together in my book that hard work that God and His servants had to do in order to let me be led by myself into salvaging faith, being born again of the Spirit, and to a personal relationship with Him.

Although I had, in the confirmation, tried to receive Jesus with the state of my mind uttered from my mouth and quite meant my message, I got to notice after years that my heart had only been half-opened for Him. I wanted to receive Jesus into my heart but I had not internalized what it should have meant in practice right after the state of mind uttered from the mouth. I would have needed a steady guidance to the Truth that one cannot even follow Jesus unless one is interested in spending time and getting to know through the Word what it actually means to follow Him. It was first through the training by the Lord's own hand that I understood what it means to kneel wholeheartedly in front of the Lord and say to the Lord: "Here is my heart and my life, take it upon you, forgive my sins so far, and teach me to live according to your will, cleansing my heart of all the slag that leads to perdition that the world has accumulated."

We may receive Jesus as sinful and unclean as we are right now, but it is our responsibility to give the Lord time to seek His will in His revelation, the Word, and to keep the Sabbath given to the Lord as a sign of the covenant. I experienced personally that as I tried to start grasping these two minimum requirements to the best of my ability, a path of miracles began that I would no longer exchange for anything this world has to offer.

Even before I was prompted by the Lord to become a prophet in 2019, the Lord had stated that my mission in writing the book was that He could no longer lead all of His elect to a saving faith along the same long road as in my case, because there would no longer be as much time to spend for all. My dear friend, for the sake of you and your beloved ones, I hope you will understand in your heart that we have come to an age about which the New Testament evangelists also declared:

"For I do not desire, brethren, that you should
be ignorant of this mystery, lest you should be wise
in your own opinion, that blindness in part has happened
to Israel until the fullness of the Gentiles has come in.
And so all Israel will be saved, as it is written:
'The Deliverer will come out of Zion, And He will
turn away ungodliness from Jacob;'"
Romans 11:25-26

Many know well the reference in the Scripts to the compliance of the number of pagans, but many will awaken too late to realize that the end of this relatively short age of grace has now really begun. I already knew we were living in a prophetically significant age, but on the whole, I too did not understand until the Lord gave this revelation, in connection with the return of the Lord, of the birth of a donkey foal, the pennant of Isaiah's prophecy and the trumpet playing now really taking place.

My friend, it does not matter so much whether one's genetic inheritance belongs to that group that the Lord is now Himself, according to His Word, collecting as a pardoned wild ass foal across congregation boundaries around the world. The invitation to join the group of the rescued is open for everyone in the world still for a while. However, that multitude raised by the Lord Himself among the various congregations around the world is of special significance in connection with the prompt to congregations, which the Lord, through His prophets, still desires to be proclaimed in these times. I have myself received that invitation, so I will write about it yet separately.

I just hope, my friend that you will open up your heart to the Lord in the next few years because the era that has begun will surprise many with its brevity. The era that has begun will no longer last for many decades, rather, we are talking about a number of years that can be counted with the fingers and toes. If you approach the Lord with all your heart during this time, there is no need to be afraid of and depressed about anything that, even after the corona, is still a tribulation for the nations of the world. Peace through the Holy Spirit is not dependent on external factors. You will understand what I mean when you can experience it by yourself by receiving Jesus into your heart and the baptism of the Holy Spirit.

However, it is important to receive the message that this Easter the Lord has asked to declare the beginning of a time when it is once again better to heed the instruction to hide in the shelter of the blood of the sacrificial lamb for the ongoing shaking of nations and for future shakings. In an unprecedented way, the Lord will start to liberate and gather together His own ones around the world in order to liberate them from nations that have drifted into apostasy and idolatry, as once from Egypt.

Unlike the first Easter, we do not need to shed the blood of animal sacrifices and brush our door frames with shed blood. Instead, it is enough for us to receive our Lord Jesus Christ into our hearts and be so involved in the protection of the blood He shed as a perfect sacrificial lamb on Easter for all of our sins.

Be richly blessed my dear friend!
Leora

Part 2

Brethren Ephraim - The Christians

WARNING! This is so-called solid food (Hebr. 5:13-14, 1. Kor. 3:1-2)

The ones exhausted by the corona time, not yet faithful, or at the beginning of their faith journey, should not continue reading from here. Instead of the good news, the text can only feel distressing in the situations mentioned above.

Those who do not blame God for the evil in the world and understand the sowing concealed by God in shaking are probably already merciful on their journey of faith with the gifts of heavenly wisdom given by the Spirit, which are a prerequisite for understanding this text and the ability to try it.

> *"All inhabitants of the world and dwellers on the earth:*
> *When he lifts up a banner on the mountains,*
> *you see it; And when he blows a trumpet,*
> *you hear it. For so the Lord said to me,*
> *'I will take My rest, And I will look from*
> *My dwelling place Like clear heat in sunshine,*
> *Like a cloud of dew in the heat of harvest.'*

For before the harvest, when the bud is perfect
And the sour grape is ripening in the flower,
He will both cut off the sprigs with pruning hooks
And take away and cut down the branches.
They will be left together for the mountain birds
of prey And for the beasts of the earth;
The birds of prey will summer on them,
And all the beasts of the earth will winter on them."
Isaiah 18:3-6

This text is a continuation of the gospel associated with the Lord's revelation of the birth and deliverance of the donkey foal in connection with His Second Coming. In connection with that revelation, the Lord prompted the proclamation of the good news to all the inhabitants of the Earth that the time of Isaiah 18:3, the raising of the pennant and the playing of the trumpet, has now begun. It is a short age when the Lord still one more time calls to follow Him and return to Him before the final execution of the time of tribulation and wrath with its judgments facing the impious.

It is, indeed, a joyful task to be involved in declaring that the Lord has raised His pennant as a sign to all the inhabitants of the Earth. It is a pennant given to mark the beginning of the whole era of approaching His return.

The Earth is already sighing its filth under our feet, and even more impiety, lawlessness, and apostasy in the world seem to be advancing (Isa. 24: 4-5, Matt. 15: 8, 2 Thess. 2: 3). Who would not rejoice at the return of the King, who will take over the whole world justly, equally, and righteously. Who, in these times of deception, disease, and pollution, would not wait for a time when the tears of the afflicted will be wiped away and those who compete for the finish will receive their rewards. Unfortunately for those who live in impiety and lawlessness as defined by the Holy Word, the end of the era, on the other hand, means the time of judgments.

The voices of the prophets around the world act as the trumpet of the Lord just like before the first coming. The messengers of the Lord forward the call of the Lord but how many will receive the call?

The Elders Are Put to Test

Honourable elders of Christian congregations, remember the nature of your Creator. His justice and fairness is unwavering.

The Lord now puts the leaders of Christian churches in the same trying as the Jewish Scriptures and Pharisees of their time.

At the time of our Saviour's first coming, only a small number of Jewish priests, rabbis, and Pharisees accepted Jesus and His invitation to follow Him. Although the Jewish priests and scribes knew the scriptures in an exemplary manner, disbelief prevailed as the Saviour, having been waited for for centuries, stood in front of them. Unbelief was not removed even by the miracles and signs performed by Jesus. It was on the contrary. The same fate befell most of the disciples who had partaken of the Holy Spirit in front of the scholars.

For centuries, Jews have got to hear from many Christians a reminder and resentment that Jews living in the time of Jesus did not realize that Jesus was truly the promised Messiah. But what about us Christians now, is my question to you, honourable leaders of Christian congregations? Will the elders of the Christian congregations even begin to try the call of the Lord proclaimed from the mouth of a Lord's servant? Are the faith and courage of today's Christian congregations better than the faith of the ancient brethren to respond to the call of the Lord, which is suddenly made again from the unexpected side as the Lord's pattern of action is?

I would like to be able to write to you this gospel sequel with the same joy as I wrote to my friend about the donkey revelation. However, it is difficult because it has been written that only a remnant of this time of the Lord's screening associated with the gospel will survive. In the midst of joy, therefore, I cannot help but feel at the same time the sorrow for that many will reject the invitation just as so many of those who sanctify God's name did at the first coming of the Lord. On the other hand, this is destined to happen so that neither of the daughters of Jerusalem will be able to boast to each other on their journey as the Lord reunites the daughters of Jerusalem into one nation, a purified bridal congregation awaiting His return. (Daughters of Jerusalem = the ancient southern people of Judah + the ancient northern Ephraim/Israel and all the people who were part of them from the gentiles).

> *"'Behold, the eyes of the Lord God are on the sinful*
> *kingdom, And I will destroy it from the face of the earth;*
> *Yet I will not utterly destroy the house of Jacob,'*
> *says the Lord. For surely I will command,*
> *And will sift the house of Israel among all nations,*
> *as grain is sifted in a sieve; Yet not the smallest*
> *grain shall fall to the ground. All the sinners of*
> *My people shall die by the sword, Who say,*
> *'The calamity shall not overtake nor confront us.'*
> *'On that day I will raise up the tabernacle of David,*
> *which has fallen down, and repair its damages;*
> *I will raise up its ruins, and rebuild it as in the days of old;'"*
> *Amos 9:8-1*

> *"'As I live,' says the Lord God, surely with a mighty hand,*
> *with an outstretched arm, and with fury poured out,*

'I will rule over you. I will bring you out from the peoples
and gather you out of the countries where you are scattered,
with a mighty hand, with an outstretched arm,
and with fury poured out. And I will bring you into
the wilderness of the peoples, and there I will plead
My case with you face to face. Just as I pleaded My
case with your fathers in the wilderness of the land of Egypt,
so I will plead My case with you,' says the Lord God.
'I will make you pass under the rod, and I will bring
you into the bond of the covenant; I will purge the rebels
from among you, and those who transgress against Me;
I will bring them out of the country where they dwell,
but they shall not enter the land of Israel.
Then you will know that I am the Lord.
'As for you, O house of Israel' thus says the Lord God:
'Go, serve every one of you his idols--and hereafter —
if you will not obey me; but profane My holy name
no more with your gifts and your idols.
For on My holy mountain, on the mountain height of
Israel,' says the Lord God, 'there all the house
of Israel, all of them in the land, shall serve Me;
there I will accept them, and there I will require
your offerings and the firstfruits of your sacrifices,
together with all your holy things.
I will accept you as a sweet aroma when
I bring you out from the peoples and gather
you out of the countries where you have been scattered;
and I will be hallowed in you before the Gentiles."
Ezekiel 20:33-41

The age that began at raising the pennant marks an era of screening before the return of the Lord, which one does not manage until they are ready to put again the Word of the Lord in front of the traditional rules created within the time of the people. This means an age as God gathers and cleanses the congregations that will enter the Lord's wedding meal into a united bride church that is acceptable to the Lord. If, accordingly, the Lord will once at His coming set everything to their place for good, the first steps have been prescribed to be taken even before the Lord's return.

> *"You have wearied the Lord with your words;*
> *Yet you say, 'In what way have we wearied Him?'*
> *In that you say, 'Everyone who does evil Is good*
> *in the sight of the Lord, And He delights in them,'*
> *Or, 'Where is the God of justice?'*
> *'Behold, I send My messenger, And he will prepare*
> *the way before Me. And the Lord, whom you seek,*
> *Will suddenly come to His temple,*
> *Even the Messenger of the covenant, In whom*
> *you delight. Behold, He is coming,' Says the Lord of hosts.*
> *'But who can endure the day of His coming?*
> *And who can stand when He appears? For He is like*
> *a refiner's fire And like launderer's soap.'"*
> *Malachi 2:17-3:2*

My sister of faith received in prayer an exhortation to be conveyed to the age: "Humble yourself to walk the way of the cross". I can only agree with the wish and pray that the elders of the various Christian congregations will be able to accept the Lord's call and humble themselves to try it in front of the Lord. Whatever your position or earthly path of education and career are, at the top of all the structures of human wisdom should be the willingness to listen to the messages of God's messengers and, according to the instruction of the Word, to try everything against the Word by the help of the Spirit. Through the ragged, the changes of the ages were communicated in connection with the first coming of the Lord, and from equally deficient vessels God's promptings are again proclaimed.

The Awakening Rain as a Reward

Before I go into more detail on the content of the Lord's invitation, I will tell about the promised prize of those who pass the screen. Part of the gospel of the beginning of a new age is that the long-awaited shedding of the Lord's heavy pre-harvest rain is really near. We are in an age when the Saints sanctified and those idealizing anti-Christian habits are only progressing deeper and deeper in their lawlessness and apostasy as revealed by the Word. In order to confirm the ability of the own ones to withstand the prescribed times of tribulation still to come, and to provide as an armoury against the spirits of evil a large-scale apostolic anointing with its miracles and signs, the Spirit set to rest in the North is awakened.

To avoid misunderstandings, I will clarify the previous. Of course, the Holy Spirit has worked in the meantime here and there, witnessing our Lord to be a living God. This presence of the Spirit, the defender of believers, the Spirit of Truth, was promised to the apostles to come. The Spirit was shed out on all those who loved Jesus on the first Pentecost (John 14: 15-17). The age that has begun is about the continuation of the Spiritual activity of the apostolic age more broadly and globally. The operation of the Spirit will be needed as the Lord frees those who seek Him by the slavery of the dark forces and by caring for the brothers and sisters in the congregation in the middle of tribulation.

Taking into account our knowledge of this age preceding the second coming of the Lord with the afflictions of Jacob, I would not want that necessary protective presence of the Holy Spirit in the middle of those times to remain unaffected by any congregation. No congregation can be built so strong in human power that without the presence of the Spirit of the Lord and the miracles of the Spirit, it would survive the future. People cannot, for example, without the Spirit in the middle of times of tribulation, be able to rely completely on the Lord for food. Food miracles will be seen where the Lord is called to help and the Holy Spirit is present. Only those congregations in which the Spirit is present as a strong advocate and encourager of those against being chosen by God are able to survive the impending age of tribulation.

Naturally, the Lord again gives people the free will to choose whether to respond to His call.

The rain soon sent by the Lord will then be directed with its richness of strong miracles there where the Lord's invitation to return to the original apostolic obedience to His Word is accepted.

And it is not only a question of the presence of miracles, but of the continued existence of congregations in general. Notice and try in Spirit the serious warning that follows the raising of the pennant and the sound of the trumpet.

> *"For so the Lord said to me, 'I will take My rest,*
> *And I will look from My dwelling place*
> *Like clear heat in sunshine, Like a cloud of*
> *dew in the heat of harvest.' For before the harvest,*
> *when the bud is perfect And the sour grape is ripening*
> *in the flower, He will both cut off the sprigs with*
> *pruning hooks And take away and*

cut down the branches. They will be left
together for the mountain birds of prey And for
the beasts of the earth; The birds of prey will summer on them,
And all the beasts of the earth will winter on them."
Isaiah 18:4-6

In His revelation, the Lord revealed to me that these verses mean, for the age to begin, what will happen to those congregations that do not respond to the call. The impervious congregations of the screening will eventually be the ones through which God accomplishes the beginning of the age of judgment. After all, it is written that the judgment begins specifically in the temple of the Lord. (thus, referring to all the congregations in the world).

As the previous warning about the gospel was particularly serious, I asked the Lord to confirm the matter requested to be proclaimed. As an encouragement, let us mention here the latest confirmation of the message, which took place on 21 March 2021. As I was in silent prayer with my co-worker given to me by the Lord, I prayed quietly in my mind the Lord to confirm the message to be proclaimed during this prayer once again. I almost felt guilty about falling into disbelief, for I had already received several strong confirmations from the Lord in this regard. After all, as part of the whole, I had recently learned why several people working on visions had received a revelation about the trumpet already for ten years. For ten years I had wondered why the Lord speaks to me about the trumpet when I have utilized my musical gifts specifically for playing the violin.

So I asked the Lord for one last confirmation and I got it. I asked if this era of the Lord's billhook really meant such serious screening for congregations, threatened by the judgment. The Lord acted immediatcly. I had not yet spoken a word to my sister of faith about that matter of the Lord's billhook. Right after I had quietly in my mind prayed to the Lord to confirm the matter by giving my sister of faith a vision for the verse, my sister of faith interrupted our silent prayer. Slightly confused by the vision she had received, she began telling she did not know anything that the Lord wanted to tell her through the vision she had just been given. She continued telling that she was shown a chainsaw, the tip of which shone with divine glory, and it swayed like a billhook in the middle of gloomy darkness. I could not, in the almost tactile presence of the Holy Spirit, be without smiling and exclaiming happily that I knew. I received my answer and I no longer hesitate to fulfil my promise to the Lord to declare all that He has given to say!

I have all the confirmation I need and I am ready to proclaim the Lord's gospel as a part of this serious exhortation to all Christian congregations in the world. Although the era includes this serious warning about screening and the call to return to the original apostolic obedience, the Word encourages to look at the raised pennant to show the wonderful goal of gathering as one Holy nation to witness the arrival of the Lord in Jerusalem:

"Go through, Go through the gates!
Prepare the way for the people;
Build up, Build up the highway! Take out the stones,
Lift up a banner for the peoples! Indeed the
Lord has proclaimed To the end of the world:
Say to the daughter of Zion,
'Surely your salvation is coming; Behold,
His reward is with Him, And His work before Him.'
And they shall call them The Holy People,
The Redeemed of the Lord; And you shall be called
Sought Out, A City Not Forsaken."
Isaiah 62:10-12

Are You Ready to Return to the Covenant?

The elders of Christian congregations, you will now find perhaps the most difficult trying of your career to put the Word of God ahead of the conclusions of human wisdom, and to possibly contest the additional challenges created by the man-made bureaucracy. What happens in a situation when leaders in the congregation with the Holy Spirit end up willing to follow God's call, but instead of spiritual leaders, lay members who are still ignorant of the Holy Spirit and the skill of trying, are deciding on doctrinal matters?

I certainly do not raise the previous concern to underestimate the spiritual capital of lay members. In fact, I am even more concerned about the situation that has been written in the press as a reality in some congregations. If the supreme spiritual leadership of the congregation does not work under the guidance of the Holy Spirit, then the principles of lay members, even though based solely on traditional rules, are the congregation's only hope of keeping the proclamation of the Truth of the Word even in its present state. Thus, there can be no congruent way to respond to the call in congregations where doctrinal matters are not in the hands of spiritual guidance alone.

The previous examples are written to encourage both elders and lay members to seriously ponder their relation to the Lord and to listen carefully to those who are trying the message in the Holy Spirit. It is an era when decisions can no longer be made under the influence of the spirit worlds that mock the Holy Spirit. It is an era when the ear scabies wished by the people and market forces cannot anymore be chosen to be more important than the announcement of the God's Holy Word. While such a strategy may seem attractive and the best in the world of earthly market forces in order to grow congregations, it would be a short-sighted and fatal misstep in the age that has begun. The Lord will no longer allow steps to be taken further from the Truth without the execution of the billhook judgment upon that congregation. Remember that the Lord never sends warnings as intimidation but as loving warnings and instructions to choose the right direction.

As the elders, according to the Word, you are responsible for the souls of your congregation. As a part of the gospel, I am not willing to quote the serious verses from the Word, which concern the duty of the elders to remain in the teaching of Will announced in the Word of God. Apostate preachers have been severely condemned in the Old Testament and the New Testament only confirms this God's line of judgment. Our Lord is the same yesterday, today, and forever.

The task ahead is therefore challenging but the reward for obedience will be great. And it is no less a matter than the matter of the life and death of many people.

Before I go through the concrete things, I have received from the Lord to convey related to responding to the Lord's call, I still want to make sure of the sufficient understanding of the connection between God's pre-written history and the present situation. I write the following because I know that church history which influences the birth of many different congregations does not necessarily address the issue from the perspective of the Word written by our Lord.

The Israeli as Branches in the Lord's Noble Olive Tree

Do you, dear reader, understand whom all the people are meant with Israeli in the title? Please understand that this means all the Jews who have received Jesus into their hearts, the descendants of the people of the ancient northern state of Israel who have received Jesus into their hearts, and the believing gentiles who have received Jesus into their hearts. Please understand that the previous triad based on the division of ancient Israel is, in fact, the same thing as the description of the divide: Messianic Jews and Christians. And if, dear reader, you have already internalized the matter under this title, you will understand that all of the above divisions are also included in one and the same definition: Israelites grafted into the olive tree include people who have taken Jesus into their heart as their Saviour (Messiah) regardless of human genetics and congregational connection.

With regard to matters relating to the beginning of the age, however, it is necessary to understand the original divide of nations made by God in the Word of the Bible, in which God divided the nations, made up of the descendants of Jacob, with the promise to Abraham into the chosen people and gentiles. It must be remembered, however, that God's promise, already made at that time as an eternal enactment, that He would also embrace those of the people who join the chosen from the gentiles. The condition was, however, that the representatives of the gentiles would also receive the acts given to the chosen people and begin to live accordingly.

> *"And if a stranger dwells with you,*
> *or whoever is among you throughout*
> *your generations, and would present an offering*
> *made by fire, a sweet aroma to the Lord,*
> *just as you do, so shall he do. One ordinance shall*
> *be for you of the assembly and for the stranger*
> *who dwells with you, an ordinance forever*
> *throughout your generations;*
> *as you are, so shall the stranger be*
> *before the Lord. One law and one custom shall*
> *be for you and for the stranger*
> *who dwells with you."*
> *Numbers 15:14-16*

> *"Also the sons of the foreigner*
> *Who join themselves to the Lord,*
> *to serve Him, And to love the name of the Lord,*
> *to be His servants— Everyone who keeps from*
> *defiling the Sabbath, And holds fast My covenant—*
> *Even them I will bring to My holy mountain,*
> *And make them joyful in My house of prayer.*
> *Their burnt offerings and their sacrifices*
> *Will be accepted on My altar; For My house shall*
> *be called a house of prayer for all nations.*
> *The Lord God, who gathers the outcasts of Israel,*
> *says, 'Yet I will gather to him Others besides*
> *those who are gathered to him.'"*
> *Isaiah 56:6-8*

Understand, as early as the time of Moses, the premise was that belonging to any congregation or genetic inheritance alone was no guarantee of salvation. At the time of the Old Covenant, the attainment of righteousness in the eyes of God was emphasized by the concrete compliance of the law given by God, although Abraham was already an example of becoming righteous by faith. Contrary to what is heard preached somewhere, through Jesus' death on the cross, the law by no means ceased to exist (Jesus even himself emphasized that not even a letter of the law will disappear, Matt. 5: 17-20).

From the teachings of Jesus, it can be said that the new covenant that came through Him, instead, renewed the covenant by modifying and supplementing the law and other provisions and instructions given by God. A good example is circumcision set by God as an eternal enactment. Even this enactment perpetuated in the Old Covenant did not disappear in the New Covenant. God does not contradecirse, and God does not have to use an eraser. Instead, as the Old Testament prophets have already declared, there would be a time when, instead of circumcision of the foreskin, one should perform the circumcision of one's own heart. In practice, circumcision of the heart means accepting Jesus as the Lord of one's life, beginning to seek, according to Jesus' prompting, the will of His Father in the Word, to listen to what the Holy Spirit begins to speak to the heart, and to grow oneself into obedience to the will of God.

Especially in all matters pertaining to the ordinances set by God as eternal, the Scriptures should be read very carefully. Which of all the laws did Jesus really change and how? Which of the laws, on the contrary, were not changed, and following Jesus by his example would, on the contrary, oblige us to comply with those laws as well? Do you love the Lord to study the ordinances He set as eternal? Have you found the Word by familiarizing with its healthy fear of God to which God Himself referred to in giving the commandments of His covenant, urging them to teach them to future generations? You have already experienced why the fear of the Lord in Proverbs is combined with the beginning of wisdom and the source of life to avoid the snares of death (Proverbs 9:10, 14:27).

"especially concerning the day you stood
before the Lord your God in Horeb,
when the Lord said to me,
'Gather the people to Me,
and I will let them hear My words,
that they may learn to fear Me all
the days they live on the earth,
and that they may teach their children.'"
Deuteronomy 4:10

The most significant change in the New Covenant, however, was that with the New Covenant we got the grace of Jesus' perfection and the work of the crucifixion to fill our own shortcomings in the attainment of righteousness. Nevertheless, this did not mean that we could in future live without the attempt to learn the will announced by God in His Word and follow, among others, the ordinances set as eternal in our lives. With the New Covenant, we truly had the grace to be saved by faith in Jesus alone, as long as we followed His example and were willing to circumcise our hearts at the pace shown by the Holy Spirit in accordance with God's will.

Following the steps of the generations of Israel after the liberation from Egypt, God found the people quite incapable of passing on the covenant instructions from one generation to another and living according to them. In the New Covenant, the Lord Himself wanted to take overall responsibility for the teaching of the circumcision of the individual's heart through His Holy Spirit. Every reborn believer knows what this means. If only for a holy day set as a covenant between the believer and God, one devotes time once a week to God in search of His will in His Word, one has certainly at some point experienced the teaching of the Lord mentioned above. In an amazing way, the Spirit himself begins to teach the texts of the Bible to a human being and step by step to increase obedience. Naturally, this does not mean that the Lord has not yet left a particular task to the teaching proclaimed from the mouth of a human being.

So who are meant by the Israeli, whom God in the New Covenant gives an opportunity to be grafted into God's noble olive tree?

Israeli refers to all people in the world who have found faith in God's only Son, Jesus Christ (in Hebrew Yeshua HaMashiach), accept him into their lives as Saviour, and begin to follow Him.

Since over the centuries, some strange doctrines have been proclaimed that only members of a certain congregation would be saved or that Jews should convert to Christianity, prioritizing the customs created during the ancient Roman Empire over the celebrations in the Scriptures, it may be worth repeating Paul's teaching about God's noble olive tree.

As Paul writes in his Epistle to the Romans, the disbelief among ancient Judah and the exile of the people of Judah soon after that marked the beginning of an age of grace for the gentiles. Right at the same time, however, Paul immediately warned the surrounding gentiles not to take pride in the mercy they had received at the expense of the stumbling of the chosen people.

Paul compared the descendants of Abraham's descendants belonging to God's chosen people into a noble olive tree that God alone decides to care for. Paul, already then, reminded the gentiles at that time that the root of the tree would never change. The tree would be the same even if God had to cut off the members of the chosen people who had drifted into disbelief from there and, in the age of grace, would also graft there branches of a wild forest oil tree, referring to the gentiles.

"For if the firstfruit is holy, the lump is also holy;
and if the root is holy, so are the branches.
And if some of the branches were broken off,
and you, being a wild olive tree, were grafted
in among them, and with them became
a partaker of the root and fatness of the olive tree,
do not boast against the branches.
But if you do boast, remember that
you do not support the root, but the root supports you.
You will say then, 'Branches were broken off that
I might be grafted in.' Well said. Because of unbelief
they were broken off, and you stand by faith.
Do not be haughty, but fear. For if God did
not spare the natural branches,
He may not spare you either. Therefore consider
the goodness and severity of God:
on those who fell, severity; but toward you,
goodness, if you continue in His goodness.
Otherwise you also will be cut off.
And they also, if they do not continue in unbelief,
will be grafted in, for God is able to graft
them in again. For if you were cut out of the olive
tree which is wild by nature, and were grafted
contrary to nature into a cultivated olive tree,
how much more will these,
who are natural branches,
be grafted into their own olive tree?"
Romans 11:16-24

But what can we say to have happened according to the history books, despite the warnings!

From the books of history we can read about the anti-Semitism toward Jews by Emperor Constantine in the 300s and its influence on the decision-making of the first ecclesiastical assemblies. In addition to the hatred of the Jews, the decision-making of Emperor Constantine was also influenced by the cost of worship of idols, which had long influenced the Roman Empire at that time. Thus, because of his own worldview, Emperor Constantine did not want to put things in the Scriptures into practice as they were written in the Word. In order to more easily incorporate Christianity into the religions that influenced the Roman Empire, through the First Synod, he established for him and his contemporaries a better nationwide version of the message of the Bible.

The content of the First Synod was thus influenced mainly by a human being who was not a scholar of the Scriptures and who showed genuine hatred towards the representatives of God's chosen people. Constantine, for example, was unaware that God had set the feast days of the Lord in His Word as His eternal ordinances to remind all future generations of the preconceived stages of His Global Plan of Salvation (through which, among other things, the probable time of the year at Lord's return can be deduced, although the year and exact timing can never be known). Thus, instead of knowing the scriptures of the Bible, Constantine made decisions on the basis of the earthly prestige available to him, e.g. marking the feasts of the Lord as feasts for the Jews only and partially replacing them with practices influenced by the idolatry rituals of the Roman Empire. Fortunately, Easter was allowed to maintain its existence although many elements of practices related to the worship of the god of fertility have been mixed with current practices.

By considering objective analysis more important than the

traditional doctrines of culture that have been passed down from one generation to the next, it can be said that something changed with the original message with Constantine. Nor do you have to read the Bible very widely when you can get an idea of God's point of view.

It is humanly understandable that these human teachings of Constantine in those centuries of dictatorship spread in that form because the common people did not have the opportunity to own their own Bible and in any way try what they had heard from the pulpit. However, God oversaw the whole and sent individual reformers to restore practices that had become increasingly distant from the Word of the Bible. No wonder, for example, Martin Luther was commissioned to declare repentance for the indulgence trade. After all, that man-born doctrine seriously offended the glory of His Son's crucifixion.

In the middle of everything, however, a lesser informed matter shall be remembered. God had already foretold that He would allow such deceptive heresies to come as part of the deportation punishments that followed the infidelity of a part of the chosen people (the northern tribes of ancient Israel, who had already been expelled from the Jews). Ezekiel 20 describes wonderfully past periods of apostasy from the people of Israel. I urge elders, as part of the ordeal of the Lord's call to be proclaimed, to pray through the Spirit throughout the 20th chapter of Ezekiel and its connection to why this call of the Lord can be answered without feeling ashamed of the heresies that have affected for centuries. One can take comfort in the opening of the eyes to the number of delusions and the existence of centuries by the fact that nothing in this world has happened without the permission of the Lord and without His prior notice. As part of the punishment for repeated missteps by the ancient people of Israel, God announced already through ancient prophets that as part of his dissolution, he would take away the Sabbath, the joy of service with its feast days, and allow new misleading commandments and rights to spread among the people.

> *"I will also cause all her mirth to cease,*
> *Her feast days, Her New Moons,*
> *Her Sabbaths — All her appointed feasts."*
> *Hosea 2:11*

> *"Also I raised My hand in an oath*
> *to those in the wilderness,*
> *that I would scatter them among the Gentiles*
> *and disperse them throughout the countries,*
> *because they had not executed My judgments,*
> *but had despised My statutes, profaned My Sabbaths,*
> *and their eyes were fixed on their fathers' idols.*
> *Therefore I also gave them up to statutes*
> *that were not good, and judgments*
> *by which they could not live;"*
> *Ezekiel 20:23-25*

> *"'As I live,' says the Lord God, 'surely with*
> *a mighty hand, with an outstretched arm,*
> *and with fury poured out, I will rule over you.*
> *I will bring you out from the peoples and*
> *gather you out of the countries*
> *where you are scattered, with a mighty hand,*
> *with an outstretched arm, and with fury poured out.*
> *And I will bring you into the wilderness of*
> *the peoples, and there I will plead My case*
> *with you face to face. Just as I pleaded My case with*
> *your fathers in the wilderness of the land of Egypt,*
> *so I will plead My case with you,' says the Lord God.*
> *'I will make you pass under the rod, and I will bring*
> *you into the bond of the covenant;*

I will purge the rebels from among you,
and those who transgress against Me;
I will bring them out of the country where they dwell,
but they shall not enter the land of Israel.
Then you will know that I am the Lord.'"
Ezekiel 20:33-38

"And for this reason God will send them
strong delusion, that they should believe the lie,
that they all may be condemned
who did not believe the truth
but had pleasure in unrighteousness.
But we are bound to give thanks to
God always for you, brethren beloved by the Lord,
because God from the beginning
chose you for salvation
through sanctification by the Spirit
and belief in the truth,"
2. Thess. 2:11-13

Now, however, we are in a time of gospel when God, through His messengers, declares that the time of that predestined punishment has come to an end. The Lord declares His mercy to ancient Israel. He is ready to renew his covenant among the Christian congregations that have taken missteps, each of which, in one way or another, bears the punishment imposed on ancient Ephraim. The Lord is ready to restore the feasts and the joy of His service to all the congregations. The Lord now asks, who is willing to humble oneself and admit the taken missteps? Who is ready to accept the invitation to return to the original covenant with Him (as it is already written to happen at the end of time)?

However, special attention must be paid by the Christian congregations to the aspect of this beginning of the age that God allowed the things set as eternal to change only among the expelled part of the Christian congregations with whom God had broken the (marriage) covenant by separation (among the gentiles, the northern tribes of ancient Israel, who had already been expelled from the Jews). It is no wonder, then, that the Sabbath, set as an eternal sign of covenant between God and His own, changed with both Constantine and later decision-makers, both when it comes to the day and practice (as the Lord announced for this to happen spiritually fornicated people in Hos. 2:11). Similarly, it is logical that the Sabbath, which serves as a sign of the covenant, has remained unchanged for millennia among the representatives of the ancient southern people, the Jews, since the habits that Jesus followed.

It is also important to remember that God does not hold people accountable if they have not even had the opportunity to receive the right teaching and knowledge. Even in past centuries, when the Lord had turned His face to a part of the people descended from Jacob through a letter of separation and the Lord allowed the proclamation of the Truth to take heresy for a predetermined period, grace still existed over those nations throughout the centuries. As promised in the New Covenant, those who have received Jesus into their hearts and sought Him from the Word have always been able to partake of the seal and salvation of the Holy Spirit. It is easy to understand when one remembers that the grace available to an individual through faith is not tied to any single earthly congregation connection. The congregation connection, on the other hand, plays an important role in finding, strengthening, and competing in faith to succeed to the finish and the promised victory prize.

Given the things revealed in God's Word about the significance of the Lord's feasts for the Lord's, own, one can better understand other missteps that God allows for Christian congregations for a period of time. It is no coincidence that the feast of the Lord, the foundation of all grace already realized during the first coming of Jesus, for the Global Plan of Salvation; the Easter, already was allowed to remain existing. Instead, it is understandable that for the people to whom the certificate of divorce was given as a sign of the dissolution of the covenant, the Lord allowed the Feast of Tabernacles, reminiscent of his birth and forthcoming return, to become an unbiblical way and time to celebrate the birth of Jesus. Those familiar with the Scriptures will understand that this also meant drifting away from a celebration that has its own important significance in waiting for the return of the Lord and celebrating the associated hope that is part of God's Global Plan of Salvation.

As for many elders, the stumbling blocks will be the same as in ancient Judah time (disbelief, pride, fear of shame and loss of status), the Lord reminds everyone of His power and promise in this matter as encouragement and consolation. This call of the Lord is not a threat to Christian congregations but an opportunity. In accordance with the verse in the book of Ezekiel quoted above, the Lord alone provided for the covering of the eyes of people and nations among both the Jews (the 1st coming of Jesus) and the present Christian congregations (the fermentations of Constantine & and their dismantling before the 2nd coming of the Lord). The Lord reminds us that no one should therefore be ashamed to feel these heresies, which have been fed mainly by national cultures for centuries. This was provided to happen for a time period.

Instead of shame, it should be gratifying that the Lord has now announced that the age of significant mercy has begun, when the Lord is ready to remove the coverings from the dispersed Christian congregations and to call everyone back to the original covenant, original obedience, and related blessings. Shame will eventually be felt in this age only by those who regard man-made traditional rules so much more important than the message of the Lord, brought by God's messenger, so that they will not even try it in the Spirit (cf. Thessalonians' description of loving injustice more than the Word of God, quoted above).

> *"'For I am the Lord, I do not change;*
> *Therefore you are not consumed,*
> *O sons of Jacob. Yet from the days of your fathers*
> *You have gone away from My ordinances*
> *And have not kept them. Return to Me,*
> *and I will return to you,'*
> *Says the Lord of hosts. But you said,*
> *'In what way shall we return?'"*
> *Malachi 3:6-7*

The Strategy Defined by the Lord for Christian Congregations

By raising the pennant and playing the trumpet, God is now calling all Christian congregations around the world to return to their original apostolic roots and renew their covenants with Him. An era has begun in which He will have mercy and betroth on the ancient people of the north, as it is written to happen through the descendants of the ancient Ephraim before the return of the Lord.

Congregations do not need to be united. Congregations do not have to be abolished and new ones do not have to be established. Instead, each pre-existing Christian congregation must consider for itself whether it will turn its gaze to the pennant, whether it will listen to the sound of the trumpet, and whether it will respond to the call.

That is why the Lord has already done what He has done. This time, He did not prepare an individual Reformer to re-create new ecclesiastical doctrines or trends. Instead, God, through His own Spirit, has awakened believers in various congregations around the world to understand the same things that have deviated from God's will over the centuries. Again, this is a matter which the Lord foretold in His Word to happen in this age:

"'Return, O backsliding children,'
says the Lord; for I am married to you.
I will take you, one from a city
and two from a family,
and I will bring you to Zion.
And I will give you shepherds
according to My heart,
who will feed you with
knowledge and understanding."
Jeremiah 3:14-15

The greatest obstacle to the conversion of the Lord's will in the congregations is probably the same to which a large number of the priests, rabbis, and Pharisees of the people of Judah stumbled. Is God more important than status, pleasing people, political and other relationships, feeling humbled in admitting that teaching has taken missteps in the passage of time from the Truth, a man-made bureaucratically intractable process, or some other obstacle? Is anything else more important than Jesus' instruction to love the Lord, your God above all else?

I know that many Christian congregations are doing strategy work again for years to come. Based on the Lord's numerous confirmations, I can assure you that no Christian congregation has been assigned more than one strategy for success in the years to come. The Lord is the head of all Christian congregations and He has prepared a workable strategy. Where His call is answered, the promise of the faithful of the book of Malachi will soon be enjoyed:

"'Will a man rob God? Yet you have robbed Me!
But you say,'In what way have we robbed You'
In tithes and offerings. You are cursed with a curse,
For you have robbed Me, Even this whole nation.

Bring all the tithes into the storehouse,
That there may be food in My house,
And try Me now in this,' Says the Lord of hosts,
'If I will not open for you the windows of heaven
And pour out for you such blessing
That there will not be room enough to receive it.
And I will rebuke the devourer
for your sakes, So that he will not destroy
the fruit of your ground,
Nor shall the vine fail to bear fruit
for you in the field,' Says the Lord of hosts;
'And all nations will call you blessed,
For you will be a delightful land,'
Says the Lord of hosts."
Malachi 3:8-12

Do you see a connection between the previous verse of Malachi and the previously quoted verse on the vines of Isaiah?

Next, I will write about the concrete first steps that the Lord individually has confirmed to me in this passage to be written as part of responding to the invitation.

1. Step - Testing the Message

Dear elders of the congregations receive my message from the Lord delivered under my mantle of the Prophet and begin to try it in the Spirit. Please do choose to try the message servants of the Lord who have experienced rebirth and who know the workings of the Holy Spirit, otherwise trying in the Spirit does not do its thing. Any member of the elders who proclaims the transformation of the Lord over millennia or the transformation of things mentioned in the Bible as sin into things favourable to God as the ages progress, is inappropriate to try the message. So be careful who you choose to try the message.

In those congregations where the message is tried and the Spirit confirms it, but the lay members decide about the doctrinal things: there may be a need for elders to first preach and teach the doctrinal bodies a comprehensive understanding of the Spirit's work and the need to put the Lord's Word in front of the ear scabies that follows the market economy at the expense of the Word. Then follows giving teaching to other congregation members, for example, by taking the next concrete step in the Lord's call to restore the Sabbath.

2. Step – Restoring the Sabbath

Bring, alongside current practices, the opportunity to gather during the original Sabbath time and its manner (Friday evening to Saturday evening).

Old traditional rule practices do not need to be abolished immediately. Let no one condemn the parishioners who, according to old practices, celebrate the holy day. Let no one also condemn those who have already responded or will respond to the Lord's call to return to original obedience. Remember that the Holy Spirit of the Lord is responsible for the timeline for each believer to write God's will in the heart through studying the Word and prayer. We cannot demand anything more from anyone.

The Lord Himself, indeed, will testify through His Spirit which habit He prefers only if the original apostolic habit, according to the Lord's message, was brought to the congregation. I refer above to the revelation I received from the Lord that in the coming rain from Him miracles (creative miracles, healings of the sick, deliverance from demons, etc.) will occur in abundance precisely where apostolic customs and obedience to the sign of the covenant, the Sabbath, are restored. Notice the connection of revelation to the Word. Many of the miracles Jesus performed took place just on the Sabbath.

I cannot think of any other reason other than the anti-Semitism that still remains since the time of Constantine in that even the mere mention of the word Sabbath seems to be a "red garment" for some congregations. The thing set for God's eternal ordinance never changed from concerning all those grafted into the noble olive tree of God.

The Sabbath is not a trivial matter to the Lord. Remember that the Lord set the Sabbath as a sign of the covenant, and in many places in the Word it can be read about the significance of the matter as a sign of obedience to the Lord and, on the other hand, curses as the cause of the Sabbath-breaking. At no point did the New Testament change that sacred rule for the Lord. Jesus' command not to condemn different practices did not mean that whatever human decision is readable by the Lord's will in the future. The follower of Jesus had to strive to follow the example of Jesus, from which one can deviate in favour of a weaker one in faith, if necessary in individual situations in the name of love (however, not everything is allowed in this situation either).

Let us repeat the basic idea of what this era means according to the Word.

We have moved to an age when God will have mercy on the remnant of Israel who received the ancient certificate of divorce. In the end, it seems quite understandable that the Lord, naturally, in this engagement of the descendants of Israel to his bride, as the first thing, calls for the return of the matter given as a sign of the covenant to those who have been pardoned. Again, we can see how God in His holiness implements the law Himself, even though none of the people can fully fulfil it.

My sister in faith described the matter finely and pragmatically by looking at it with the help of a parable given by the Lord Himself.

After all, marriage between a man and a woman is in many ways recognizable from the Word of the Bible as a symbol of the relationship between the Lord and His bridal congregation. It is understandable that biblical marriage is therefore also quite holy to the Lord. As the Lord's return and the expected wedding feast approach, it is natural for the bride to be beautified for the wedding feast (cf. the exhortation of Christian congregations to purify their doctrines and return to original obedience in the era that has begun). From this perspective, the Sabbath can be thought of as a regular meeting day between the Lord and his fiancé. If the bride arrives to meet the future bridegroom each time on a different day than the terms of the covenant have agreed, it is understandable that the promise of the covenant will stand alone because of the Lord's forbearance and grace. This perspective is good to take into account when considering in the congregations how encounters between the Lord and people and the testimonies of the Holy Spirit about the living God could be increased.

To see the miracles of the Spirit on Sabbaths in the congregations, however, make sure that the work of service in Sabbath gatherings is performed by reborn servants who are faithful to the Word of the Lord. It is useless to accuse the Spirit for fleeing a place and the absence of miracles and signs from congregation life if persons who declare things defined as sin in God's will to be allowed to people in modern times are called to represent God. Our God of Abraham, Isaac, and Jacob, Yahweh (YHWH), is the same yesterday, today, and forever.

If your congregation has a part of a wild ass foal made by God at this time, give them the floor. For this purpose, God has, hundreds of them even in Finland, if not thousands, already sown in the various congregations.

Although the Lord is an orderly God, the Lord did not set formulas to bind the various activities of the Spirit on the appointed holy day, the Sabbath. Imagine new joyful gatherings where Jesus' examples of the purpose of the Sabbath are fulfilled: diaconal family connection, interactive Bible study, breaking bread & wine as a memorial meal, joyful & Spirit-present praise & thanksgiving, opportunity for people to meet God through the testimonies of the Spirit (e.g. prayer service).

YHWH would also like Christian congregations to make sibling connections with Jewish congregations. Restoring the Sabbath is a great opportunity to create a connection between the siblings of ancient Zion. Where Christians can invite their Jewish brothers and sisters to congregations to share practices that have been preserved for millennia and contain many interesting details opening up the Word of the Bible, a common Sabbath spending would be an opportunity for Christians to reciprocally convey the good news of the gospel to the Jews (Messianic Jews have actually already received Jesus to their hearts).

A very important part of restoring the Sabbath is also to return to the congregations a teaching, to the members of the congregations, about what the families' own responsibility is for the Sabbath, in addition to the things they receive through the congregation connection. In addition to receiving the teachings of the Word on the Sabbath, encounters with the Lord through the work of the Holy Spirit, and a loving and caring congregational family connection, the Sabbath has also its significance for the family well-being and blessings. In addition to taking care of passing on the knowledge of the Word to their children, at least on the holy days, in order to increase their knowledge of our Heavenly Father and His Son, families should gather in one way or another to thank and praise the Creator for the good things in life by being together.

In the service of the Lord, especially on the weekly Sabbath, the call from the Lord to serve Him with joy should be visible. As an example to families, I have conveyed a music video related to Joshua Aaron's happy Sabbath wish for the desired Friday night atmosphere:

https://youtu.be/IIwCDYWOEQ4
(Found by Google: Joshua Aaron Shalom)

The Lord's desire to restore joy and happiness to His service therefore applies not only to the churches but also to the believers' own acts of faith and family connections.

Where Christian congregations have had the joy of taking the gospel of Jesus to as yet unknown Jewish brothers and sisters (reference to Jews and Christians as daughters of Jerusalem), in the beginning of the era should Christian congregations and Christian families reciprocally learn from the Messianic Jews about the service of the Lord with joy and according to the Word, by celebrating the Sabbath and the feasts of the Lord.

The Lord's invitation to return to the original covenant with Him means the period of the Reformation before the Lord's return, in which the Lord, through His invitation and the associated sieve, will sweep away e.g. the heresies that came into the life of faith and the doctrines with Constantine.

It is worth noticing that even Jews have been framed by their own age-old tradition on the Lord's Word, but ways to spend the Sabbath and the Lord's feast are still based on the times and habits of the Word. However, unlike Christians, most of the ways that emerged as the traditional rules of the Jews have a biblical basis and they beautifully only deepen the instructions of the Scriptures.

Since the stigmatization of the Lord's feasts and Sabbaths to be habits belonging only to the Jews, which has been influential since the days of Constantine, is still strongly influenced in many Christian congregations that have exerted since Constantine's synod, I repeat once again that the restoration of apostolic habits to the Christian congregations is not a matter of conversion to Judaism but of a necessary predestination by the Lord to the original obedience to the Word before the return of the Lord.

"And the Lord spoke to Moses, saying,
'Speak also to the children of Israel, saying:
Surely My Sabbaths you shall keep,
for it is a sign between Me and you
throughout your generations,
that you may know that I am the Lord
who sanctifies you.
You shall keep the Sabbath,
therefore, for it is holy to you.
Everyone who profanes it shall surely
be put to death; for whoever does any
work on it, that person shall be cut off
from among his people.
Work shall be done for six days,
but the seventh is the Sabbath of rest,
holy to the Lord. Whoever does any
work on the Sabbath day,
he shall surely be put to death.
Therefore the children of Israel
shall keep the Sabbath,
to observe the Sabbath throughout
their generations as a perpetual covenant.
It is a sign between Me
and the children of Israel forever;
for in six days the Lord made the heavens
and the earth, and on the seventh day
He rested and was refreshed.'"
Exodus 31:12-17

The Sabbath was instituted as an eternal covenant between the Lord and the Israeli. With the New Covenant, Jesus again only supplemented the Sabbath guidance. Jesus did not change the time of the day consecrated to God to another. I will not go into this in more detail here, but let me mention, noticing all the possible readers that even the death penalty was not abolished by the New Covenant, even though life is no longer intended to be deprived with the death penalty. The constant neglect of the Sabbath, on the other hand, will inevitably eventually lead to spiritual death, which in turn will have its own consequences in the post-bodily period as well. The death penalty is a good example of what kind of changes the Word refers to, for example the transformation of the law from the Law of Flesh into the Law of Spirit. The death penalty itself did not disappear either, although instead of a carnal death, eternal ordinance changed with the New Covenant to concern spiritual death that means, to be separated from God and the salvation available through Jesus.

3. Step – Restoring the Feast of Tabernacles

Alongside Christmas, which was born as a tradition of the people, restore the biblical way to celebrate the birth of the Lord and the anticipation of His return, as God ordained as eternal in His Word to all who are grafted into His noble olive tree. In fact, nowhere in the Bible is there even a request to celebrate the birth of Jesus, but by studying the Word, one can understand that God has set the Feast of Tabernacles (Sukkot) to be eternal during the celebration of the Lord's coming to Earth. Those who already understand the cyclicality of God's Plan of Salvation know that it is no coincidence that the Lord was born on Earth for the first time during that autumn feast, and, on the other hand, it is celebrated annually as a prelude to the wedding feast of the return of the Lord (+ in addition to the former, as a memorial service in connection with historical events).

As with the Sabbath, the old practices of traditional rules do not need to be abolished immediately. Let no one begin to condemn the congregation members who will continue to celebrate Christmas in honour of the birth of Jesus. Let no one begin to condemn those congregation members who have already been called by the Lord through His Spirit to change as part of the restoration belonging to the age. Remember that the Holy Spirit of the Lord is responsible for the timeline for writing His will to each heart. However, the Spirit cannot do his work in those congregations that do not respond to the Lord's call and do not even allow believers to return to the original practices indicated by the Word.

Just as with Easter, God in His command to celebrate the Feast of Tabernacles had both historical and future significance. On the one hand, God wanted to set it up as a celebration set from generation to another to commemorate the past with joy (things set to be remembered after the liberation from Egypt). On the other hand, He wanted the Feast of Tabernacles to be celebrated as an eternal ordinance as a reminder of things still to be promised as part of God's Global Plan of Salvation.

In contrast to Easter, the event of the Feast of Tabernacles concerning the Global Salvation Plan has not yet taken place. It has been right also in the past centuries to sing in the Christian congregations about the anticipation of making it to the Lord's wedding meal. The misstep, however, has been that a human being, who did not know the significance of the feasts instituted by the Lord, was allowed to remove God's eternal ordinance reminiscent of the Lord's return and the expected wedding meal from those following Jesus. It is no coincidence that God set the celebration of the birth of His only Son for that feast. And it is no coincidence that for the Second Coming of His Son, He wanted to prepare His elect in the form of that feast of joy year after year for the return of His Son to Earth. Do you again recognize the exact planning of the Lord in the parallels of the first and second coming of the Lord. I myself agree with the well-known notion of the Scriptures that one year, when God's elect in festive costumes and multi-day parades have gathered, our Savior will also return in the middle of the Feast of Tabernacles. After all, Jesus himself gave that little hint in response to his brethren going to the Feast of Tabernacles:

"Then Jesus said to them,
'My time has not yet come,
but your time is always ready.
The world cannot hate you,
but it hates Me because I testify of it
that its works are evil. You go up to this feast.
I am not yet going up to this feast,
for My time has not yet fully come.'"
John 7:6-8

Those who become acquainted with the Word of the Feast of Tabernacles, which is given as a model for the wedding of the Lamb, will probably quickly find a connection between the Lord's Day in connection with the return of the Lord and the Great Day of Atonement (Yom Kippur). Personally, I usually refer only to the time of the Feast of Tabernacles, because the return of the Lord (on the great Day of Atonement, Yom Kippur) is so closely connected to the beginning of the long-awaited Wedding Feast of the Lamb (Feast of Tabernacles). It must also be borne in mind that, in order to avoid people starting to guess the exact days and years, the Lord has allowed lunar calendars to be calculated slightly differently from the Hebrew calendars to determine the annual festivities. It is therefore more important to understand the significance of the annual celebrations instituted by the Lord as part of the Lord's Global Plan of Salvation than the exact dates. Understanding the Feast of Autumn is a necessity in order to understand the significance of the era that has begun for every individual believer.

The Word warns seriously against thinking of the return of the Lord without checking the state of our own faith as just a joyful wedding-related matter. The day of the Lord signifies great joy and the beginning of the wedding feast for those who have been ready to bleach their garments according to Jesus' instruction. For the impious and those who walk in lawlessness, it is a day of judgment instead of joy. Because the Almighty knew that big missteps and scattering would leave many souls in false assurance of salvation (not just for Christians), YHWH ordained this prophetic time of playing trumpet (the first of the Feasts of Autumn) to call for purification for the impending return of the Lord and the wedding of the Lamb.

The Lord is now calling the Christian congregations, all of which are more or less influenced by the teachings of the ancient emperor Constantine, to give their congregation members the opportunity to be among those who are already ready for the joyful celebration on the coming day of the Lord's return, according to the Lord's wish.

The significance of the Feast of Tabernacles for the Lord can also be seen in many eschatological verses of the Word. It is no wonder, then, that the Lord commanded it to be included as part of His call in this beginning of the age.

4. Step – Making an Improvement from the Substitution Theology

If your congregation is one of those congregations where the Israel mentioned in the Word is preached only to mean present-day Christians or that only our congregation members or denomination will go to heaven, the time has come to shake off all such leavening. The time has come when the elders of the congregations must understand Paul's description of God's noble olive tree and the message of Ezekiel 37. A time has begun when the elders of the congregations must understand that the root of God's noble olive tree remains unchanged in the promise made to Abraham by the blessing of His descendants and the strangers who joined them.

Let us still repeat that although God once expelled ancient Judah and Ephraim (Israel) from the Promised Land, God never dismantled the special status of those peoples in His Global Plan of Salvation. God also described very early on how, as part of the Plan of Salvation, the gentiles will have the opportunity to join those nations (and not the other way around).

In the wake of the anti-Semitism of ancient Constantine, many churches have modified the message of the Bible so that the church congregations would form a new Israel and even the Jews would have to join them for salvation. To be saved, the Jews only need to receive the Lord Jesus into their hearts as their Saviour, nothing more. The Messianic Jews have already done so. It has been a joy to follow the constant increase in the number of Messianic Jews and the way in which they live their faith in the presence of the Holy Spirit with the same joy of original obedience revealed in the Scriptures.

As stated earlier in the text, God allowed these missteps of the leavening of compensatory theology as a pre-written part of punishment as well as because the current Christian congregations would not be able to boast alongside Jewish sisters and brothers. The Spirit should give an understanding of the matter to see God's equal treatment of the daughters of Jerusalem. As much as Christian congregations have criticized Jewish habits, some of which are their own cultural heritage rules created on top of Biblical Word practices, in this age the eyes of Christian congregations receiving the Lord's invitation will be open to their own man-made traditional rules affecting for centuries that have seriously diverged from the Word of the Bible.

Thus, neither of the daughters of Jerusalem (Judah & Israel) will be able to boast on the journey including flounders when the Lord returns. More important than the flounders is the arrival and the fact, that with both remnants, a large number of believers from gentile nations will also return (this is especially well shown in Ezek. 37). Thus, genetic inheritance still does not matter in terms of acceptance of faith. Instead, genes matter as to how God will use these descendants of the ancient people of Israel in each way to implement the Global Plan of Salvation in different ages.

5. Step – Making an Improvement from the Supergrace Preach

If your congregation preaches the departure of God's law with the New Covenant and super grace, in which God forgives anything without any requirement to even try to become acquainted with and obey God's will through the Word, it is time to shake off the teaching of that leaven.

Grace and salvation are truly available to all, but the grace of Jesus' cross work should not be mocked. It is scary to listen to and see how half of Jesus' own words about His suffering and grace coming through the crucifixion have very often been cut off in sermons, thereby also leaving people in false assurance of salvation. Jesus himself said after he rose from the dead and appeared to his disciples:

> *"Then He said to them, 'Thus it is written,*
> *and thus it was necessary for the Christ to suffer*
> *and to rise from the dead the third day,*
> *and that repentance and remission of sins should be*
> *preached in His name to all nations,*
> *beginning at Jerusalem.'"*
> *Luke 24:46-47*

The former is a very different matter from preaching: all sins so far are forgiven, continue the same way as before!

Of the sins, only the blasphemy of the Holy Spirit is mentioned as a sin that cannot be forgiven, not even by the grace enabled by the crucifixion of Jesus. Numerous other verses from the Bible testify how other sins can be forgiven, but the condition is a desire to repentance. Preaching super grace shockingly decries the crucifixion of Jesus.

The starting point for the manifestation of God's power in the congregations is to preach the grace that will come through the suffering and death of His Son as Jesus Himself has commanded. The elders should be able to give people the right hope of God appearing in people's lives by teaching guidelines for living according to God's will. The elders should be able to tell what sin is in God's eyes according to His word and what is not. The elders should be able to teach parishioners how important part studying the Word of the Bible is to the life of a believer, even then once a week on the holy day as set as eternal ordinance. The elders should be able to teach that if only obedience to God is sought and He is sought in the Word, He will at some point surely give His Spirit in support of the change in repentance. The elders should be able to teach how God does not require one-time success in change or one-time learning of His will, but it is about a step-by-step growth process in the life of an obedient believer. The elders should be able to teach congregation members that if only they try to get to know God by becoming acquainted with the Word, the Holy Spirit will undergo a circumcision of the heart at each of their own pace, enriching them with miracles and signs.

It is not in vain the Word calls the journey to the saving faith a competition, and gives an example of foolish and wise virgins. In this regard, as part of Friday or Saturday Sabbath gatherings, begin to teach the congregation members what it really means to follow Jesus (including Jesus' obedience to the Father's will + Jesus' instruction to follow His example).

The neglected need for preaching repentance and the ignorance of God's will expressed by God's Word has led to a worrying and sad increase in self-righteousness among people. As the importance of studying the Word is not taught, neither the character and the will of God can be known, nor the Holy Spirit can speak to people through the Word. Many drift into life in constant sin and even try to buy righteousness in the eyes of God with monetary gifts. In practice, money is used to try to do good deeds by buying a good conscience to atone for sins that are not even attempted to repent, even if they may be known as sins at heart. The elders should have the courage to teach that no matter how good the deeds made possible by money are abundant elsewhere, or even if millions are handed over to the churches, sowing lies, hatred, deception, and injustice at the same time one is likely to be left out of saving faith. And it is not always just a matter of the person himself, but in the worst case, a person, unknowingly, still leaves to their posterity the burden of sin that followed from sin, with its curses. Especially in these past decades of prosperity permitted by God, there would have been a need to teach what Jesus meant by his parable of the camel going out of the eye of a needle. How many souls have been left without salvation because no one has dared to preach about the need to repent and the insignificance of money in circumcision of the heart. Grace is available to all, but how many are finally, for receiving the grace, ready to give their hearts to the Lord to be shaped by the humility to seek God's will and to genuinely attempt to live obediently to God's Word. While faith alone saves, faith without deeds (according to God's will) can be dead and leave people in false assurance of salvation. Indeed, in ancient times, the apostles even gave a rich man the opportunity to preach the Truth boldly:

> *"But Peter said to him, 'Your money perish with you,*
> *because you thought that the gift of God*
> *could be purchased with money!*
> *You have neither part nor portion in this matter,*
> *for your heart is not right in the sight of God.*
> *Repent therefore of this your wickedness,*
> *and pray God if perhaps the thought of your heart*
> *may be forgiven you. For I see that you are poisoned*
> *by bitterness and bound by iniquity.'"*
> *Acts 8:20-23*

So shake your congregation out of rebellion by revealing God's will to enable people to repent to be forgiven of their sins.

Also shake your congregation out of rebellion against the word law. After all, it is only a matter of God's loving instructions that show the purpose of righteousness. Thank God that He gave His only begotten Son so that no believer would perish, even if they were only at the beginning of their efforts to follow Jesus' example in doing God's will. However, everyone should have the opportunity, according to Jesus' command, to know the will of His Father and the opportunity to repent so that the grace of the crucifixion may be the atonement for all sins. God does not require much of us. There should be a desire in the heart, even once a week, on a day set by God, to seek God and His will in the Word. God has promised to receive everyone who seeks Him (Luke 11: 5-13). Many accuse God for not answering prayers and lacking miracles and signs, but how many have first tried to find God in the Word as the Word teaches.

What After the First Steps?

The previous First Steps announced by the Lord are the starting points on which everything is based. If you are faithful when it comes to the teaching of the need to restore the Sabbath and repent as part of the forgiving of sins, the Holy Spirit, as part of His duties, will do other work in hearts and congregations.

Furthermore, for the sake of certainty, it should be noted that the beginning of this age does not mean that the Lord will immediately gather the remnant of Israel into present-day Israel. However, in the Spirit, I urge you to carefully consider the description of riding a donkey during the Easter time. There is a stage going on when the apostles prepared by God around the world will release that donkey mare and donkey foal and thus pave the way for the Lord. However, the Lord asked us to remind you not to fall asleep under the interpretation that the whole restoration would take place only after His return. He is already ahead of us all the time, as it is written. We know that the details of biblical parables and events have amazingly accurate meanings. In connection with the approach of the return of the Lord, it is worth considering what guidelines could be inferred from the fact that in the Easter tableau the donkey's head first enters the gates of Jerusalem (supporting the view of other places in the Word).

Indeed, it has been established in my heart through many prayers and revelations of the Lord that, as with the Jews, the remnant of Israel, with its associated gentiles, will already begin its return to the Promised Land before the return of the Lord. At some point in the middle of that process, one year during the Feast of Tabernacles (or actually during the Day of Atonement just before the Feast of Tabernacles, also referring to the different methods of calculating the time of the feasts in the Hebrew calendars), the Lord will return to the Mount of Olives as written. It is worth noting that according to the information I once heard on the radio about the tribes of the ancient northern people, the descendants of the Manasseh tribe have already returned from India. The partial return of the descendants of ancient Israel already before the return of the Lord can, therefore, be seen to have started in our time.

> *"'I will surely assemble all of you, O Jacob,*
> *I will surely gather the remnant of Israel;*
> *I will put them together like sheep of the fold,*
> *Like a flock in the midst of their pasture;*
> *They shall make a loud noise*
> *because of so many people. The one who breaks*
> *open will come up before them; They will break out,*
> *Pass through the gate, And go out by it;*
> *Their king will pass before them,*
> *With the Lord at their head.'"*
> *Micah 2:12-13*

Warning to the Elders of Finnish Congregations

Although we Finns have a reason to rejoice for the independent land we have received through the miracles of God, and for its beautiful meaningful form, there is no more room for pride and spiritual blindness. In my autumn article on the website, I described last summer in connection with a message I received from the Lord, how the people of Finland, the leadership of the country and the people's church have slipped into a state of serious apostasy over the past decades. Although, on top of that, we still shine at number one in international headlines in terms of worldly standards, the state of our nation, by the standards of God's trial, actually corresponds to the state that already led to the punishments of the ancient northern state of Israel.

While the outer shell is largely made to shine in the headlines of the media guided by the power of money, there are many things beneath the surface that are partly visible and partly very skilfully hidden to elevate the wrath of the Lord. This is how it was in the time of ancient Ephraim. When the apostasy goes far enough, not even the grievances are brought up anymore, but they are skilfully tried to hide (media game, censorship, etc.). Since my writing last autumn, the amount of apostasy just seems to have progressed even in our beloved homeland. After all, God especially follows the realization of righteousness and justice in the nation.

So I have been instructed by the Lord to put those dimensions of Ephraim's apostasy into another very precise concrete writing, after which it should be unclear for none as to why punishments can soon be seen to come if repentance is not made even after the last exhortation. I must proclaim that message with as heavy a heart as Elijah and Amos did during the time of Ephraim. God, as mentioned in the book of Isaiah, has already put on his armour of vengeance (Isaiah 59:14-17). However, he waits until the last, but the time for repentance in Finland is really running out.

But as in the days of Ephraim, though God raises his prophet to warn and exhort repentance, the people with ears will not hear, nor will the people with eyes see. As during the apostasy of Ephraim, the spiritual blindness of the people will eventually lead to shakings of the nation.

The only good thing about the situation in Finland is that the Lord has spoken to me and confirmed to me what will happen in Finland in the following years is great for arousing the knowledge of God and the fear of God and reverence for God among other gentiles. Do you see the connection again to the time of Ephraim. Before the shakings came upon Ephraim, the nations beside them were instructed to observe the events in order to learn about the dominion of the God of Abraham, Isaac, and Jacob in this world.

In practice, the alternatives for Finland now are for the nation's leadership to wake up in the last time given to repentance and, as in the war years, to declare to the people the need for repentance, return to their knees and cry out to the Lord for help. Of course, as in our struggle for independence, God would respond to prayers and cry with abundant nation blessing again. It must be remembered that in the cause of God in the terms of the state of the nation is by no means only the leadership of the nation, but the leaders of all the congregations in terms of righteousness.

Another option is a path without repentance and turning to God. It is the path of the tear valley of Agar with its shaking, which God, in the middle of the weeping of the nation, turns to salvation for many, while restoring the nation to its original healthy fear of God. I believe that Ýou too have a hunch which path in the light of the history of the nations is more probable.

So it may really happen that the Maiden of Finland is not allowed to maintain her beautiful form only as the nation's apostasy progresses. I can only say, like the Old Testament prophets, that MAYBE God will still change His judgments if we repent at the last moments at the nation's leadership and the congregations rejoice the Lord by responding to His call.

Even if the judgments come, there is always a comforting side due to God's way of doing things. Although our country could no longer celebrate as the bridal congregation, the sign of which was given to us the form of our country, those who have been screened among the nations responding to God's call, will come to celebrate as a bride.

In Summary and as an Encouragement

We have arrived at a special period predestined by the Lord at the end of the grace period. At the same time, however, the call contained in the gospel signifies an age of screening in which the Lord will exercise the justice with the nations and congregations that have drifted into apostasy. Receive this message of mine from the Lord and try it. Remember that only the Truth revealed by His Word is valid for God as defence in justice. Do not go in front of the Almighty with the human doctrine for which there is no basis in the Bible. Do not go in front of the Almighty, succumbing to the things that Peter warned about:

"knowing this first: that scoffers will come in the last days,
walking according to their own lusts, and saying,
'Where is the promise of His coming?
For since the fathers fell asleep,
all things continue as they were
from the beginning of creation.'
For this they willfully forget: that by
the word of God the heavens were of old,
and the earth standing out of water
and in the water, by which the world that
then existed perished, being flooded with water.

But the heavens and the earth which
are now preserved by the same word,
are reserved for fire until the day
of judgment and perdition
of ungodly men."
2. Peter 3:3-7

"and consider that the longsuffering
of our Lord is salvation—
as also our beloved brother Paul,
according to the wisdom given to him,
has written to you, as also in all his epistles,
speaking in them of these things,
in which are some things hard to understand,
which untaught and unstable people
twist to their own destruction,
as they do also the rest of the Scriptures.
You therefore, beloved, since you know
this beforehand, beware lest you also fall
from your own steadfastness,
being led away with the error of the wicked;
but grow in the grace and knowledge of
our Lord and Savior Jesus Christ.
To Him be the glory both now and forever.
Amen."
2. Peter 3:15-18

Those who are willing to humble themselves in front of the Lord to admit the missteps of our ancestors affecting our cultures and teachings and thus passing back under His wand, He will restore to His protective covenant. Rebellious and human doctrines, as well as human desires that are made more important than His Word, He will separate from the crowd at the end of this age. (Ezek. 20: 33-41)

Thus, be bold shepherds and respond to the Lord's call to return to the original covenant with our Creator. Study, try and start to bleach the wedding garment of the congregation by purifying to the obedience to the Lord's Holy Word of the apostolic time.

The Lord will be with you mightily in change through His Spirit and guide you forward only if you show through the first steps that you receive the call in your congregations.

"And blessed is he who is not offended because of Me."
Matthew 11:6

With blessings and praying the strength and courage of the Spirit of the Lord in your work,

Leora

Part 3
Brethren Judah – The Jews

"Again the word of the Lord came to me, saying,
'As for you, son of man, take a stick for yourself
and write on it: 'For Judah and for the children of Israel,
his companions.' Then take another stick and write on it,
'For Joseph, the stick of Ephraim, and for all the house of Israel,
his companions.' Then join them one to another for yourself
into one stick, and they will become one in your hand.'"
Ezekiel 37:15-17

My dear Jewish brothers and sisters, writing this chapter seems like the most challenging task of all in the whole message. If only one manages the challenging school that often precedes the Lord's prophetic vocation assignments, will it then be easy to be the Lord's messenger after all. One should only focus on emptying all of one's own thoughts and focus on acting as an intermediary for the Lord.

With this chapter, I found myself in an unexpected situation. First, in a familiar way, the Lord instructed me to write to the Jewish brothers and sisters what He has given to write to them. Then the surprise came. The Lord went on urging me to also write what I would like to say to you as my sister through my own feelings and thoughts. In my morning prayer, I expressed my concern to the Lord asking whether the instruction certainly was from You, the Lord. I told how I want to be only a messenger of His words. Elohim repeated the request to begin writing the chapter by writing to you as your sister.

Alright.

As Your Christian Sister at the Door of Your Synagogue

Dear Jewish sisters and brothers, I begin to write to you viewed as your sister through an ancient promise to Abraham, descended from the descendants of ancient Ephraim, who was already expelled from Israel before Judah.

I feel like I am standing outside your synagogue as your long-lost sister without daring to knock on the door. I hear through the door how the joyful songs of the Sabbath cease, and the study of the books of Moses begins at the point assigned to that week. As I raise my hand to knock, I drift for a moment to reflect on the teaching I got myself as a child from the Scriptures. How lost I was as a Christian until about the age of 40 in knowing the nature and will of our God. As a Christian, the teaching in my childhood in my congregation was mainly focused on going through the earthly life and activities of the Son of God (Immanuel) who came among us. I knew the Son of God, our Savior (Hamashiach), but not the original instructions set by His Father to His elect. However, our Savior Yeshua obediently carried out the will defined by the Father in the Scriptures and commanded His example to be followed. Yeshua fulfilled the law, although He also brought some changes to it in the New Covenant made possible by the Almighty through Him. After all, our Savior Himself was a

Jew, as evidenced in the Gospels where He richly quotes and explains the teachings of the Scriptures.

The hand that almost already knocked on the synagogue door drips back down. Through the Judaism descended from our Savior, David's line of descend, I drift into thinking of the anti-Semitism that has spread in the world even among Christians. How contradictory! In His Scriptures, YHWH stated that he allowed the descendants of ancient Ephraim to aberrate, but how great the price of that cover placed on the eyes of Christians has been. Dear Jewish brothers and sisters, I am truly sorry for what you, as a nation scattered around the world, have had to experience among different nations. Sorry for our ancestors. Sorry for those who do not understand what some are still doing today, whether they are Christians or not.

Our Almighty Father YHWH would not have originally wanted His elect to be back then divided into two nations. Like a punishment by an angry Father for His wrangling children who are rebelling against His instructions, he allowed the anti-Semitism, for a time, to remain as a shameful burden all the way to this day, even between the descendants of the same ancient kingdom.

Ephraim, who had previously been expelled to Judah, from which Christianity sprung, was given the privilege of receiving Yeshua first in his life. In his great plan, YHWH allowed the eyes of the people who were first expelled, and, of the gentiles to be the first to open to the understanding of Yeshua as the Messiah promised by the Scriptures. However, as our own cover for our eyes and touchstone, we obtained for Christians that serious heresy that sows anti-Semitism that violates brotherly and sisterly love through the power of the ancient emperor in the 300s (in previous chapters, I have discussed the subject in more depth as part of the Lord's announced call to repentance for Christian congregations).

Again in my imagination I see how I would hopefully raise my hand after gathering courage at the synagogue door. I would like to knock and, as the door opens, begin to rejoice with my hands as a support for my incoherent verbal explanation, the Gospel announced by the Lord. As serious and terrible as all things that have happened have been, I would like to outright shout out that YHWH has now promised to remove those covers off of the eyes of both siblings. We can once again be the one group of original elected ones who together gladly praise our Almighty God, the Lord Sebaot, and await the impending return of His Son with the founding of the Kingdom!

Dear Jewish sisters and brothers, if only everything was as easy as the coming of an individual Christian to the door of the synagogue in her sisterly love to make peace with a common meal and joining the merrymaking. Through a speech strongly confirmed by our Almighty, I know that this reconciliation, as well as the restored connection between the sisters, is what our Heavenly Father wants to give to the siblings in the age that has begun. But which of us are willing and able to receive the gospel?

Please forgive and open your hearts to the gospel of Yeshua

Thank God, now in my writing I can return from my own feelings to His promptings.

In the previous chapter, I have announced the invitation to the Christian congregations contained in the age of purification that begins with the playing of the Lord's trumpet. The time of screening has begun, which neither all Christian congregations will pass. In the teaching of stamping the feasts of the Lord as feasts belonging only to the Jews, transferring the original holy day to another day instead of the Sabbath, and e.g. the timing of the birth of Jesus at Christmas is a matter of human doctrine and traditional rules that have influenced cultures for centuries. Without the help of the Holy Spirit, even individual Christians cannot shake off the cover of their eyes, even though the Lord has made it possible as part of the age to bring about the unification of His people described in Ezekiel 37. Where the elders of the congregations have an important role to play in the age, the Lord still invites every believer to do their part to turn back to Him.

Those Christians from whose eyes the Lord has already removed the cover can even be persecuted within Christianity for converting to Judaism, or other such. After all, it is by no means a question of converting Christians to Jews or converting Jews to Christians. Instead, it is a matter of the Scriptural work of the Almighty to cleanse and reassemble His own, once again together, joyfully awaiting the arrival of the promised Savior.

YHWH is ready to confirm the call of the message to have come from Him through His Holy Spirit to concern everyone. However, there will be many who reject the message even before the message is tested. Some Christians will also turn their backs to the message, for example, because they have not been taught the workings of the Holy Spirit and therefore do not even know how to try the message and ask and receive answers from the Lord. Some may turn their backs as they are offended by the sudden questioning of the doctrines and set-ups of the fine systems formed by civilization. For both Jews and Christians, therefore, the era means not only the gospel but also a test of knowing God and faith.

I deeply appreciate the continued way among Jews to pass on the teachings of the Scriptures to following generations. When I personally experienced the Lord's great mercy by the removal of the cover on my eyes for the serious delusion allowed for Christians by YHWH, I can imagine how strange the centuries-long conversion of Jews by Christians has seemed. Why should Jews give up the scriptural feasts, holy days, and other biblical customs that the Lord has ordained them for His own as eternal enactments? I could imagine the confusion to have existed, however, as to why there have been signs among Christians of the supernatural activities of the Holy Spirit of Almighty God, even though they have not been as obedient to the instructions of Scriptures in many aspects. As a mother of several children, I cannot help but smile at this stage how Heavenly Father has viewed the situation in his father's role among siblings stumbling in their different ways. One blames the other without seeing their own fault and the other, of course, on the contrary, just blames the other for slightly different things.

I rejoice at how the Jews have carried the Word in its value and succeeded to pass on important teachings from one generation to the next. I believe, therefore, that Judaism has survived through challenging eras even without its own land. With regard to the Global Plan of Salvation of the Almighty, one can see how YHWH, through you Jews, has maintained the things and practices given as unbroken eternal ordinances, e.g. the command to celebrate the annual feasts of the Lord that was given after leaving Egypt. As a Christian, I feel deep sorrow for what Christians have lost for many centuries within their faith, and thus their lives, as a consequence to the loss of these biblical celebrations and other instructions. For Christians, however, they were meant as children of our same God YHWH.

Dear Jewish brothers and sisters, after all, there are two things the Lord has prompted to be proclaimed to you regarding the age that has begun.

The first is forgiveness.

Forgive Christians for the actions of past centuries and the false conversion to Christianity. You really do not need to turn to anything from Judaism, but only to receive the Truth cherished and proclaimed by Christian generations that Yeshua really was and is, the Savior promised by our Almighty YHWH in the Scriptures.

The second thing, in fact, was already mentioned at the same time. Just as Heavenly Father now tests the consent of Christians to humble themselves to listen and learn from the biblical feasts and Sabbath the Jewish brothers and sisters have preserved as the eternal enactments of the Lord, Our Almighty Father will test the Jews in this age by urging you to listen to the gospel message that Christians have passed on from generation to another for centuries. This is important because only those who have received Yeshua in their heart and have achieved the seal of the Holy Spirit in the heart will get through and survive the following age at last.

The wisdom of our Heavenly Father as a parent cannot be stopped. Can you see, the Almighty of sovereign humanity has transported the descendants of the chosen ancient Israel to an era from which the descendants of the ancient chosen people cannot continue apart as momentarily lost sisters without reconciliation.

The era of Ezekiel chapter 37 has really begun, when on the holy Sabbath set by the Lord Sebaot the Holy Word is rejoiced as a whole reunited nation. Just as there is no Son without the Father, there is no New Covenant with its gospels without the Scriptures of the Old Covenant. One of the sisters has been honored to cherish the foundation written in the Scriptures and the other sister has instead received the gospel laid upon the foundation. In the age that has begun, through the hand of the Lord, everything is united into one whole.

The era does not mean founding new congregations, the abolition of the old ones, or the amalgamation of congregations. It is a matter of turning the gaze of all the congregations waiting for the return of our Savior Yeshua to the same glory, hope, and purpose. I hope to see Jews in the beginning of the era visiting Christians and vice versa. While Jews can come to tell about the generations-old biblical feasts and spending Sabbath that the Lord meant even for Christians, Christians can reciprocally share that important gospel message passed down from generation to generation on the Sabbath. In the age that has begun, the Lord will powerfully testify of His presence with the testimonies of the Spirit through miracles and signs.

Now is the time for the daughters of Zion to make atonement, to purify themselves, and to rejoice together to await the return of our Savior and to invite others to be saved!

Hallelujah!

Epilogue

For readers who have already had an understanding of the exemplary nature of the Lord's feasts included in the Scriptures as a description of the stages of the Almighty's Global Plan of Salvation, may have, when reading the book, already awaken to the contact with the content of the message proclaimed in this book and the connection between the day of the trumpet playing, which is a part of the autumn festivities.

Dear readers, we have the tremendous privilege of living in a very prophetic time. Where the first coming of Jesus carried out the spring feasts of God's Global Plan of Salvation (Easter/Pesach, the Feast of Unleavened Bread/Chag Ma'Hazot, Counting of the Omer/Sefirah, Pentecost/Weekly Feast/Shavuot), for all of the Lord's own, the feasts of autumn prescribed in the Scriptures are related to the Second Coming of the Lord. The Feast of Trumpets (Yom Teruah/Rosh Hashanah) begins the three festivities of autumn, which, in addition to the joyfully awaited return of the Lord, are accompanied by anxiety and judgment on those who walk in the world in impiety and the lawlessness described by the Lord in His Word.

For readers who are even more unfamiliar with the idea of the Lord's Feasts as a model for the Lord's Global Plan of Salvation, I urge you to read Keijo Lindeman's concise description on the subject on the Israel-Apu ry website attached to the supplementary materials.

The era that has begun, on one hand, is a great cause for joy. The beginning of the day already associated with the day of the Lord signifies the true approach of the return of our Savior. Jews and Christians will awaken to ancient brother- and sisterhood as the Lord, in this age, removes the covers He has set from the eyes of the daughters of Zion and those who have joined them from the gentiles. At the same time, according to the Scriptures, a land already sighing under our feet for filth is waiting for the cleansing of our Savior from all evil and filth in connection with the return.

On the other hand, the gospel of the beginning era includes a more serious message. The voices of prophets around the world sound like trumpets of the Lord, as a sign for the beginning age so that still each called person would awaken to review their own state on the journey of contending for the life crown. It is time for every believer to check the amount of oil in their lamp of the Holy Spirit and, on the other hand, to consider whether they have succeeded in passing on the keys of saving faith to their descendants and those close to whom they would like to celebrate the crown of life with in the Lord's Kingdom.

As with the fulfillment of the Spring Feasts, the era of the fulfillment of Fall Feasts in the Global Plan of Salvation will not be long. In any case, in connection with the return of the Lord, it is no more about centuries, rather years, at most decades. The day of the trumpet playing has been given as a joyful feast to the beginning of the age, as it is again an expression of the love of our God YHWH. He never brings anxiety before having warned His loved ones through His messengers and conveyed His instructions on overcoming the challenges ahead triumphantly.

For the review of the state of faith at the individual level, the purification, and the strengthening of faith required in the age,

YHWH gave a separate message to proclaim. It can be read in the third section of the salvation message, a book called For Your Victory (Voitoksesi). YHWH gave it to be proclaimed so that no believer would have the same fate at the arrival of our Savior, as in the teaching of Jesus the one arriving to a wedding without a wedding garment had (Matt. 22). There is still a moment left in the age of grace and some time to seek God, to be born again of the Spirit, to be baptized, and to nourish the Spirit by the Holy Word in order to whiten one's garments for the approaching wedding of the Lamb.

With blessings,
Leora

Additional Material

Israel-Apu ry

Keijo Lindeman's concise description on the Lord's feasts as a description of the stages of the Almighty's Global Plan of Salvation (in Finnish):

https://israel-apu.fi/kirjoittaja/keijo-lindeman/herran-juhlat/

Something similar in English for example by Wycliffe:

https://www.wycliffe.org/feast/7-feasts-that-point-to-christ

Medialähetys Sanansaattajat ry

An interesting and comprehensive explanatory work of the Word of the Bible, prepared by radio pastor Jukka Norvanto and his team members Elina Karonen and Merja Kauppinen as auditions (in Finnish):

https://rkk-sansa.net/kuuntele/

The roots of the Finnish Bible from Cover to Cover (Raamattu kannesta kanteen) program go back to America and Sansa's international cooperation with TWR. TWR360 offers similar Bible study programs in a number of different languages:

https://ttb.twr.org

Taivas TV7

Note! If copying the web addresses below feels laborious, the alternative is to search for the program for viewing on the website www.tv7.fi. Programs can be conveniently found by going to the Sheet (Arkki) section of the website and searching for the program there by the name of the program or series of programs using the Find function.

A series 'Kuningaskunnan tuuli' by Ari and Mia Valkeakari: The great sign (Rev. 12) in the sky on September 23, 2017 and interpretations of its meaning are described, among others at (partly in English, mostly in Finnish).

https://www.tv7.fi/arkki/kuningaskunnan-tuuli/suuri-merkki_p58824/

The restoration described in the Word of the Bible has also been made into an interesting series of programs. I attach here couple of links for You. Please, remember that God has given the crown of being 100% right only to His Son Jesus. All the words, teachings, and prophecies of God's servants are always meant to be tested (as even all my words in this book). As described in the Word, God also deliberately reveals the whole with time as if a puzzle is being done with one piece at a time. Therefore, do not be surprised if there are small differences in teachings and interpretations. If you study the places of the Word and pray the wisdom of the Holy Spirit, you will not grasp all the differences, but you will still find that everything is pointing to the same goal.

A series on restoration by Kimmo Juutilainen (in Finnish, English subtitles may be available later):

https://www.tv7.fi/arkki/ennalleenasettaminen/sanan-ennalleenasettaminen-kimmo-juutilainen_p17087/

A series on restoration by Keijo Lindeman (in Finnish, English subtitles may be available later):

https://www.tv7.fi/arkki/kaiken-kohdalleen-asettaminen/mita-ennalleenasettaminen-tarkoittaa_p33232/

As an interesting additional material regarding the significance of the Easter and the Feast of the Lord, I will include a link to the recent TV7 program series Kaksi Pääsiäistä (Two Easters). The program series deals nicely with Easter from both Old Testament and New Testament perspectives. I still remind you that while the series reveals the celebration of the holy day postponed in the footsteps of Constantine to the supposed resurrection day of Jesus, it does not remove the Lord's revelation to celebrate the holy day at the time appointed by the Lord. Of course, the Day of Resurrection is also important, and as the series finely points out, the hint given by the Lord about the resurrection on Sunday was already visible in the Old Testament. However, even in the Old Testament, that day was to be celebrated in addition to the Sabbath, and nowhere in Word can be found the permission to replace the day set as a sign of the covenant entirely with that other day.

A series by Jouko Jääskeläisen, Andre Tischer as a guest (in Finnish, English subtitles may be available later):

https://www.tv7.fi/arkki/kaksi-paasiaista/osa-1-3-uhri_p80034/

Thomas Nelson Publishers

The New King James Version of the Holy Bible (NKJV) was commissioned in 1975 by Thomas Nelson Publishers. It is available at site Bible Study Tools:

https://www.biblestudytools.com/nkjv/

Notes

Lightning Source UK Ltd.
Milton Keynes UK
UKHW020628070721
386770UK00012B/921